D1519689

BATTLES
THAT CHANGED THE WORLD

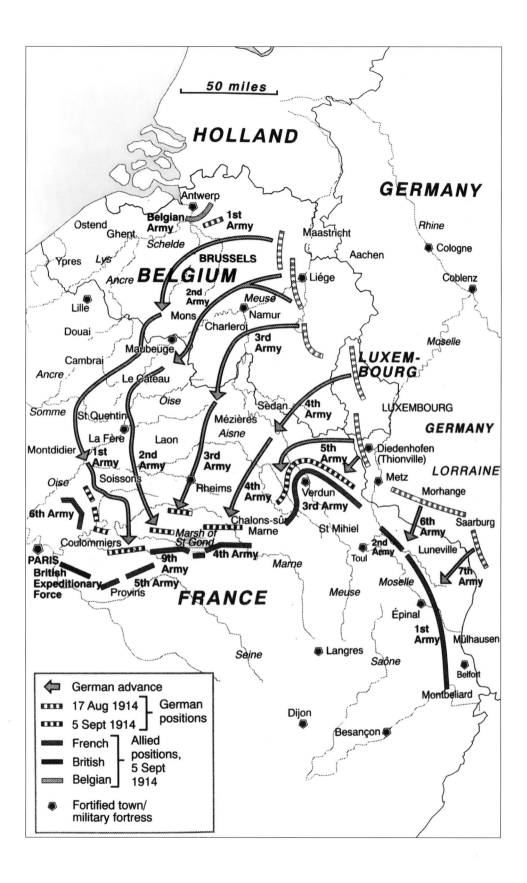

BATTLES
THAT CHANGED THE WORLD

THE FIRST BATTLE OF THE MARNE

EARLE RICE JR.

CHELSEA HOUSE PUBLISHERS
PHILADELPHIA

Cover: This photo shows German shock troops about to advance on the western front. This type of carefully planned, segmented attack was typical of the Germans, but as the war progressed both the Allied and Central Powers became extremely wasteful of human life.

Frontis: This map shows the progression, and the stop, of the German advance into France. On the left-hand side, notice the curve to the east made by the German First Army. That move allowed the French and British to counterattack at the Battle of the Marne.

CHELSEA HOUSE PUBLISHERS

EDITOR IN CHIEF Sally Cheney
DIRECTOR OF PRODUCTION Kim Shinners
CREATIVE MANAGER Takeshi Takahashi
MANUFACTURING MANAGER Diann Grasse

STAFF FOR THE FIRST BATTLE OF THE MARNE

EDITOR Lee Marcott
PICTURE RESEARCHER Patricia Burns
PRODUCTION ASSISTANT Jaimie Winkler
COVER AND SERIES DESIGNER Keith Trego
LAYOUT 21st Century Publishing and Communications, Inc.

http://www.chelseahouse.com

First Printing

1 3 5 7 9 8 6 4 2

Library of Congress Cataloging-in-Publication Data

Rice, Earle.
   The First Battle of the Marne / Earle Rice, Jr.
      p. cm. — (Battles that changed the world)
Includes bibliographical references and index.
   ISBN 0-7910-6685-1
   1. Marne, 1st Battle of the, France, 1914 —Juvenile literature. 2. World War, 1914-1918—
Juvenile literature. I. Title. II. Series.
D545.M3 R53 2002
940.4'21—dc21

2002001614

TABLE OF CONTENTS

August 1914:
Sabbath at Mons

British soldiers, called "Tommies," march to the front lines of the war in France. Their smiles suggest these men have not yet seen combat.

"I think I know the situation thoroughly and I regard it as favorable to us," wrote Field Marshal Sir John Denton Pinkstone French on the night of August 21, 1914, in a report to British war minister Field Marshal Horatio H. Kitchener. Sir John, the stocky, white-haired, mustachioed commander in chief of the British Expeditionary Force (B.E.F.) in France, went on to predict that his forces would not engage in any serious fighting before the 24th. He was wrong.

On August 4, Great Britain had joined with France and Russia in the war against Germany and its allies. The war—World War I—was called the "Great War" by citizens at a time when even the wildest imaginations could not conceive of a still greater war yet to come. Eight days later, Sir John's B.E.F., comprising one cavalry division and four infantry divisions, began landing at Le Havre, Boulogne, and Rouen, France, and heading toward Mons, Belgium.

Major General Sir Charles H. Fergusson's Fifth Division completed the last leg of its journey in timeless infantry fashion, marching 40 miles from the railway stations at Le Câteau to Mons in two days. Young officers encouraged their troops to sing on the march and strains of "Tipperary" and other marching songs preceded them as they crossed the Franco-Belgian border. Cheers of Belgian villagers offered slight comfort to the parched and weary infantrymen as they trudged past.

"It was so very hot," one British soldier recalled later. "We met a trickle of civvies [civilians] coming the other way and I saw little carts being pulled by dogs. My feet were hurting and I thought it was a funny sort of war."

The British soldiers all but wilted in stiff serge uniforms that soaked up the rays of the scorching midsummer sun and then soon turned wet with their sweat. And their feet sizzled inside boots made of reversed Indian cowhide, packed in grease at issue and kept supple thereafter with regular applications of dubbin boot dressing. Adding to their discomfort on the march, the infantrymen carried their personal gear on their backs, which weighed upwards of 80 pounds or more, along with a standard issue of 150 rounds of .303-in ammunition in square canvas pouches strapped to their waists. Most important to all British infantrymen of their time, they carried, slung on their shoulders, the Short Magazine Lee-Enfield (S.M.L.E.) Number 1 Mark III rifle. Before entering battle, they would shed all equipment except their rifle and bayonet, ammunition, a water bottle, and a haversack with rations and eating utensils.

As the "Tommies" trod the country roads north of the border and drew ever closer to Mons, the southward trickle of civilians turned into a torrent of humanity. "Refugees swarmed past us all day," one private of the Sussex Regiment noted in his diary. The flood of fleeing civilians did not augur well for what lay ahead of the British contingent.

The B.E.F. arrived at the Mons-Condé Canal in Belgium on August 22. Marshal Sir John French immediately deployed his forces in defensive positions. Major General Sir Horace Lockwood Smith-Dorrien's II Corps (Third and Fifth Divisions) took up positions along the canal. The waterway was 64 feet wide and 7 feet deep and ran west to east from Condé to Mons for some 20 miles in an arrow-straight line. Smith-Dorrien's Third Division also filled in a salient (a two-mile-wide by one and one half-mile-deep projection) formed east of Mons where the canal looped northward.

Lieutenant General Sir Douglas Haig's I Corps (First and Second Divisions) extended the defense line in a southeasterly arc, intending to link up with General Charles Louis Marie Lanrezac's French Fifth Army on the B.E.F.'s right flank. Marshal French held Major General Edmund Henry Hynman Allenby's cavalry division in reserve near Quiévrain. Sir John expected to march northward, level with Lanrezac's Fifth Army on his right, and throw the Germans out of Belgium. But the gods of war frowned on his expectation.

Marshal French set up his headquarters (H.Q.) at Le Câteau. On the morning of the 22nd, Sir John, unsure of Lanrezac's intentions and plan of attack, set out toward the French commander's headquarters at Philippeville. He did not look forward to a meeting with Lanrezac, as he held the Frenchman in low regard. In their first meeting, Lanrezac had greeted him harshly. "At last you're here. It's not a

Belgian civilians flee the combat area. Belgium's neutrality had been guaranteed by all the Great Powers since 1839. Germany's violation of that guarantee enraged the British public and brought Great Britain into the war.

moment too soon," his French ally said. "If we are beaten, we'll owe it to you." The annals of time do not chronicle Sir John's response.

The two men developed an instant mutual dislike and distrust. Neither man spoke the language of the other; but tones of voice, personal demeanor, conflicting views, and translation difficulties engendered a reciprocal antagonism that would blemish all of their future relations and attempts at cooperation. Today, however, no further unpleasantries would pass between them. A steady stream of *poilus* (French slang for soldiers; literally, "hairy ones") retreating southward blocked northbound progress to Philippeville. Sir John returned to Le Câteau.

Later that morning, the old field marshal received reports of skirmishes between British and German cavalry units to the northeast. British aerial observers confirmed the reports that afternoon. He soon received another report, delivered by Lieutenant Edward L. Spears, his liaison officer with the French Fifth Army: The Germans were hammering Lanrezac's army. One of Lanrezac's staff officers accompanying Spears then stepped forward to deliver his commander's request for the B.E.F. to attack north of the Sambre and relieve the pressure on the Fifth. Such a move might expose his entire flank to attack. Sir John rightly declined but pledged to stand firm at Mons for 24 hours.

That night, the 22nd, Sir John summoned the leaders of both corps and the cavalry division to Le Câteau. He told them that "owing to the retreat of the French Fifth Army" the British offensive would not take place. At that point, except for its Xth Corps, which was not next to the B.E.F., the Fifth Army was not in retreat. But Sir John, it seems, had to blame someone—and who better than Lanrezac? A day earlier, Lanrezac had blamed Sir John's late arrival for his own failure to take the offensive.

Sir John went on to inform his commanders of his promise to defend their present positions for 24 hours. He estimated the strength of the enemy in front of them at no more than two army corps plus cavalry, a force roughly equal to his own. His appraisal of the enemy fell far short of reality. At that moment, General Alexander von Kluck's

German First Army was bearing down on the British with four corps and three cavalry divisions—160,000 men and 600 guns (cannons). And one of Kluck's two reserve corps was within two days' march of the B.E.F. whose total strength numbered 70,000 men and 300 guns. In short, the Germans fielded a superiority of manpower over the B.E.F. of 2.3 to 1, supported by twice as many guns.

When General Smith-Dorrien returned to his II Corps headquarters at 2:30 A.M. on Sunday, August 23, he immediately ordered the bridges over the canal to be prepared for demolition. Later that morning, he issued instructions for the bridges to be destroyed on divisional order "in the event of a retirement being necessary." Had Smith-Dorrien's sensible precaution been exercised by many of his French counterparts, the French might have lessened their appalling casualty rate of August 1914. But they had not.

At about 6 A.M., Marshal French motored to Smith-Dorrien's headquarters, where Haig and Allenby joined him. The marshal and his three commanders reviewed their situation and all concurred that their positions were adequate to withstand an attack. Sir John left his chief of staff behind with "full instructions as to arrangements which must be made if a retreat became necessary," then drove off to Valenciennes to witness the arrival of the Nineteenth Infantry Brigade. The brigade was a new unit assembled from rear-area units. Shortly after the marshal's departure, Kluck's First Army struck.

The Sabbath at Mons began like most other Sundays. Black-clad villagers in the nearby mining communities, as yet unaffected by events beyond their control, answered the call of church bells that rang out across a pastoral setting and shattered the hush of a gray, drizzly morning. The Belgian churchgoers spent the rest of the day in Hell.

Paul Maze, a French painter serving as an interpreter

Marshal Sir John French commanded the British Expeditionary
Force. He and French General Lanrezac had repeated conflicts and
misunderstandings.

for the British, reported the civilian scene when the
Germans drew close and firing erupted: "[I]n a few
seconds all these civilians were fleeing along the roads
while the invasion, creeping up like a tide, steadily
gained ground. In their Sunday clothes, carrying in their

hands their feathered hats which they had not stopped to put on, the wheeled perambulators [baby carriages], wheelbarrows, bicycles, and anything on wheels, and fled with their babies and terrified men."

Kluck directed his forces first to the weakest part of Smith-Dorrien's defense line, the salient projecting northward to the east of Mons. In the mist and rain of that Sunday morning in August, Captain Walter Bloem of the Twelfth Brandenburg Grenadiers became one of the first Germans to experience the devastating effects of the Short Magazine Lee-Enfield rifle in the hands of expert riflemen: "No sooner had we left the edge of the wood than a volley of bullets whistled past our noses and cracked into the trees behind. Five or six cries near me, five or six of my grey [uniformed] lads collapsed in the grass. . . . Here we were as if advancing on a parade ground . . . away in front a sharp, hammering sound, then a pause, then a more rapid hammering—machine guns!"

In fact, he was not hearing machine guns at all. What Bloem and his Grenadiers were encountering was the "15 rounds a minute," rapid—and deadly accurate—firing of the First Battalion, Queen's Own Royal West Kent Regiment, banging away so fast with their Lee-Enfields that the Germans mistook rifle for machine-gun fire. "[The German] losses were very heavy," General Smith-Dorrien recalled later, attesting to the effectiveness of his marksmen, "for they came on in dense formations, offering the most perfect targets, and it was not until they had been mown down in thousands that they adopted more open formations."

To the west of the salient, Kluck's III and IV Corps emerged from the woods and struck the center and left of Smith-Dorrien's II Corps. At Jemappes, 210 men of the First Battalion, Royal Scots Fusiliers, backed by a single machine gun, held more than 2,000 gray-clad troops of the German Sixth Infantry Division at bay all afternoon. Artillery shells

Taken on August 3, 1914, this photo shows French soldiers about to be transported to the war in Belgium. On that very same day, the French poet Charles Peguy wrote in his journal, "Whoever failed to see Paris this morning and yesterday has seen nothing." War enthusiasm ran high at the start.

filled the air for hours. British artillery spotters crouched for cover in coal slagheaps that speckled the mining region. "The enemy turned the coalyard where we sheltered into what looked like an active volcano," commented Second Lieutenant Kenneth Godsell of the Royal Engineers. "Bits of shrapnel and debris were flying everywhere."

By three o'clock that afternoon, the B.E.F. had withstood continuous shelling and unrelenting German attacks for six hours. But the enemy onslaught had taken a heavy toll and the Tommies began blowing up bridges in preparation for retiring. Nor did the Germans escape lightly, as evidenced by Captain Bloem's recollection of the battleground after the fighting: "Wherever I looked, right or left, there were dead and wounded, quivering in convulsions, groaning terribly, blood oozing from fresh wounds. They apparently knew something about war, these cursed English."

At 3:10 P.M. at the B.E.F. general headquarters in Le Câteau, Marshal French was dictating a message to General Lanrezac: "I am prepared to fulfill the role allotted to me when the Fifth Army advances to the attack. In the meantime I hold an advanced defensive position extending from Condé on the left through Mons to Erquelines. . . .

"I am now much in advance of the line held by the Fifth Army, and feel my position to be as forward as circumstances will allow, particularly in view of the fact that I am not properly prepared to take offensive action until tomorrow morning." Clearly, Sir John, who was still contemplating offensive action the next day, knew nothing of the battle that had been raging all day at Mons. And while Sir John completed his dictation, General Smith-Dorrien ordered his corps to retire to new defensive positions two to three miles behind the Mons-Condé Canal.

At sundown, German buglers, much to the amazement of the embattled British, sounded the call to cease fire. By then, Bloem's regiment was "all to pieces." The Twelfth Brandenburg Grenadiers had lost 25 officers and 500 men. Bloem would later remember his battalion commander telling him, "You are the only company commander left in the battalion . . . the battalion is a mere wreck, my proud, beautiful battalion." Total German casualties were never fully disclosed, but military historians estimate their losses at nearly 5,000 on the day. British casualties totaled 1,600 killed, wounded, or missing.

Sir John arrived at the front just in time to hear the German bugles calling for a cease-fire. A few minutes later, news arrived from Allied commander in chief General Joseph Joffre informing him that the estimate of German forces facing the B.E.F. had been increased to three corps and three cavalry divisions. The news ended any thought of still mounting an offensive.

Lieutenant Spears arrived at 11:00 P.M. with worse news yet: General Lanrezac had ordered a full retreat of the Fifth Army. Field Marshal Sir John Denton Pinkstone French now found himself and his besieged expeditionary force fully exposed to attack from the front and from both sides by a numerically superior enemy.

So ended the Sabbath at Mons on August 23, 1914.

Old Rivalries and New Alliances: The Origins of World War I

This famous painting shows Wilhelm I of Prussia about to receive the crown of German Emperor. Otto von Bismarck, Wilhelm's key policy-maker, is in a white uniform right of center. The ceremony took place in the Hall of Mirrors at Versailles, at the end of the Franco-Prussian War of 1870-1871.

The battle at Mons on August 23, 1914, constituted the first British engagement of what history now generally refers to as World War I, or the First World War. Before the advent of World War II, or the Second World War, its predecessor was known most often as the "Great War" or the "War to End All Wars." The causes of the so-called Great War continue to generate pulp for the paper mills of historians and powder for the conjectural cannon of armchair generals. Most students of times past can agree, however, that the motives that drove the participants in the Great War were—as was the war itself—less than great. Many historians place a vindictive France at or near the top

of any list of World War I's causative factors.

The roots of history grow deep and tangled, especially those of European nations and cultures. To lend a manageable limit to the roots of World War I, historians often elect to begin with the Franco-Prussian (or German) War (1870-71). The war was fought primarily because of a Prussian effort to install a Prussian prince on the throne of Spain. France felt threatened by the possible shift in the balance of power. French militarists considered the French army to be sufficiently strong to defeat the Prussians handily. The Prussians vested similar confidence in their own army. When France declared war, the two armies were put to the test on the battlefield. The Prussians rapidly mobilized for war and prevailed with startling efficiency, humiliating the French army in a lightning campaign that lasted a mere six months.

On May 10, 1871, by the Treaty of Frankfort, a vanquished and embittered France agreed to cede the northeast provinces of Alsace and Lorraine to Germany and to pay an indemnity (compensation) of five billion francs ($1 billion). "Having provoked the 1870 war, France deserved ignoble defeat," observes military historian S. L. A. Marshall. "She got it." But not all German leaders agreed with the harsh reparation terms.

Prince Otto von Bismarck raised strong objections over the annexation of Alsace-Lorraine. He expressed grave concerns that France would never forgive it, but insistent German military leaders overruled his protests. The militarists who invoked the demands felt willing to risk France's enduring enmity. Field Marshal Count Helmuth Karl Bernhard von Moltke (the Elder), chief of the German general staff, predicted, "What our sword has won in half a year our sword must guard for half a century." Moltke's prophecy missed the mark by only seven years when his nephew, General Count Helmuth

Johannes Ludwig von Moltke (the Younger), pointed the German sword at Paris in 1914.

The Prussian victory in 1871 yielded far-reaching and long-lasting effects. It led to the unification of Germany and the creation of the German Empire, to the demise of Napoleon III's Second French Republic (and French dominance in Europe), and to the establishment of the Third French Republic. With Napoleon III unable to defend the sovereignty of the Papal States—territories in central Italy over which the pope claimed dominion—Italy annexed them, thereby completing its unification. The crushing Prussian victory also reaffirmed the German peoples' confidence in the Prussian military system, a collective faith that remained a dominant force in German society until 1945.

Beyond all else, in the view of many, the German annexation of Alsace-Lorraine lit the flame of resentment and shame in the souls of the French that only the recovery of their lost provinces would extinguish. Although peace prevailed in Europe for 43 years after the Franco-Prussian War, it was an unstable and uneasy peace. Germany's mounting imperialism and France's determination to regain Alsace-Lorraine kept the two nations continuously poised for a resumption of hostilities.

Perhaps Victor Hugo, France's great poet, dramatist, and novelist, best captured the prevalent French sentiment of the time: "France will have but one thought: to reconstitute her forces, gather her energy, nourish her sacred anger, raise her young generation to form an army of the whole people, to work without cease, to study the methods and skills of our enemies, to become again a great France, the France of 1792, the France of an idea with a sword. Then one day she will be irresistible. Then she will take back Alsace-Lorraine." Germans thought otherwise.

Germany had emerged from the Franco-Prussian War as the dominant power in Europe and intended to maintain its dominance. Bismarck, an astute politician who served as German chancellor from 1871 to 1890, understood France's bitterness and cautioned his compatriots that a "generation that has taken a beating is always followed by a generation that deals one." He also recognized that strength usually lies in numbers and engaged in a series of political and diplomatic maneuvers that gradually culminated in the military coalition of the Central Powers—Germany, Austria-Hungary, and Italy—known as the Triple Alliance. Each member nation promised to assist the others if one or both became involved in war with two major powers of the world, but would remain neutral in the event of war with one. For example, Italy pledged to remain neutral in a war between Austria-Hungary and Russia but would fight in a war between the Central Powers and a Franco-Russian foe.

France, not to be left behind by its hated rival, allied itself with Russia and Great Britain to form a similar military alliance called the Triple Entente. ("Entente," is French for "understanding" or "intent"; thus "Triple Entente" translates into three parties pledged to support the national interests or intentions of one another.) This trio of Entente nations later became better known as the Allied Powers, or the Allies.

Britain, which had held to a policy of nonalignment over the years, was the last of Europe's so-called great powers to enter into a military alliance. As an island nation, with the world's greatest navy to protect itself, Britain did not wish to become embroiled in continental conflicts. The British attitude began to change, however, when Wilhelm II succeeded his father as kaiser (emperor) of the German Empire in 1888. The new kaiser began a naval building

This photo was taken as Franz Ferdinand and his wife Sophie walked to their car in Sarajevo. Franz Ferdinand was the nephew and heir of Emperor Franz-Joseph, who had held the Austrian throne since 1848.

program intended to challenge British supremacy on the high seas.

"The formidable shape and threat of that navy began to impress Britain right after the turn of the century," writes S. L. A. Marshall. "Then, in a flamboyant speech at Reval in 1904, Wilhelm styled himself as the Admiral of the Atlantic. Englishmen began to ask what use Germany had for such a navy other than to break

England's sea power." A fair question, Marshall might have added, that nourished Britain's need to seek allies else risk standing alone in an increasingly hostile European environment.

That same year, Britain, via an *entente cordiale* (cordial understanding) with France, loosely attached itself to the Franco-Russian combine—a mutual assistance pact that had been formed in 1891 and modified in 1893. The pact called first for the two parties to consult if either party were threatened by aggression; it was then modified to require them both to mobilize if any member of the Triple Alliance should take the first step. Mobilization would later become a key factor in the outbreak of hostilities.

In 1912, Britain further aligned itself with France when the two governments agreed to consult and decide what action to take in the event that the general peace was threatened or if either nation had cause to fear an unwarranted attack. This slender thread that bound the two nations promised nothing of great significance from the beginning. But it added a further complication to an already complex system of military alliances, a system that many discerning observers believe to have brought on the war that they were intended to prevent.

As a case in point, military historian John Keegan writes: "The net of interlocking and opposed under-standings and mutual assistance treaties—France to go to war on Russia's side and vice versa if either were attacked by Germany; Britain to lend assistance to France if the vital interests of both were judged threatened; Germany, Austria-Hungary, and Italy (the Triple Alliance) to go to war together if any one were attacked by two other states—is commonly held to have been the mechanism which brought the 'Allies' (France, Russia, and Britain) into conflict in 1914 with the 'Central Powers' (Germany and Austria-Hungary)." The alliances themselves did not start World War I, of course, as Keegan goes on to point out, but they insured that it would spread to all of the strongest nations, or "Great Powers," of Europe and ultimately involve 30 nations in theaters around the globe.

Two years before the start of World War I, chief of the German general staff Helmuth von Moltke (the Younger) wrote, "The outbreak of a general war will, as a result of the alliances on both sides, follow on a collision between two of the great powers of Europe." And that it did, fueled by a continental ambiance of animosity and reinforced by a rampant sense of nationalism.

In the four-plus decades since the Franco-Prussian War, national identities and awareness had become deeply ingrained in the collective psyche of the European masses. Everything from military spending to colonial competition provided ample opportunities for expressions of national pride. Of course, there were always the alliances and treaties to fuel the energies of opposing patriots.

As Barbara Tuchman writes, "Europe was a heap of swords piled as delicately as jackstraws; one could not be pulled out without moving others." Others have described the Europe of 1914 as an armed camp or a powder keg waiting to explode. As summer approached, all that was needed to thrust the swords, trigger the guns, or light the fuse to the powder keg was a provocative event of some kind. On June 28, 1914, just such an event took place.

That morning a young Serbian nationalist named Gavrilo Princip shoved his way through a crowded street of Sarajevo, jumped aboard a royal motorcar, and shot Austria-Hungary's future emperor, the Archduke Franz Ferdinand, and his wife, Sophie, to death.

Princip, a 19-year-old patriot or terrorist, depending on the point of view, belonged to a secret society known as *Ujedinjenje ili Dmrt,* the Black Hand (or more accurately, "Union or Death"). The society wanted to terminate

Serbian nationalist Gavrilo Princip is seized by police, minutes after he shot and killed the archduke and his wife. The assassination set in motion a train of threats, counter threats, and mobilizations that culminated in the start of World War I, just one month later.

Austro-Hungarian rule in the Balkans and unite the South Slav peoples into a federal nation. Princip believed that the assassination of a member of the Habsburg imperial family was an essential first step. Austria-Hungary's military clique had sought an excuse to mount a small punitive war against Serbia for years. They wanted to teach the discontented and disruptive Serbs a lesson. Princip's act gave them the excuse they needed.

Although a subsequent inquest revealed no connection between Princip and his companions and the Serbian government, the military clique in Vienna refused to accept the results of the investigation. General Franz Conrad von Hötzendorf, chief of the Austro-Hungarian general staff, viewed the archduke's assassination as "not the crime of a single fanatic; assassination represents Serbia's declaration of war on Austria-Hungary. . . . If we miss this occasion, the monarchy will be exposed to new explosions of South Slav, Czech, Russian, Rumanian, and Italian aspirations. Austria-Hungary must wage war for political reasons." Austro-Hungarian Foreign Minister Count Leopold von Berchtold agreed that war was necessary.

Backed by Hötzendorf, Berchtold persuaded old Emperor Franz Joseph to ask Germany to support a hostile Austrian action against Serbia. Emperor Wilhelm II's reply on July 5, which came to be known as the "blank check," proclaimed that Austria "could depend on the complete support of Germany."

On July 23, heartened by the Kaiser's assurance of German support, Berchtold sent a 10-point ultimatum to Serbia, demanding a reply within 48 hours. Meanwhile, Austria-Hungary and Germany began quiet military preparations short of mobilization. Serbia accepted all but one of Berchtold's demands, a condition that violated the Serbian Constitution and that would strip Serbia of its sovereignty.

In its response to Berchtold's ultimatum on July 25, Serbia respectfully suggested that the point in contention be further discussed before The Hague Court of Arbitration. (The Hague, Netherlands' seat of government, is also a center of international law and corporate administration.) On July 28, one month after the assassination of the archduke, Austria-Hungary declared war on Serbia—and the pledges of Europe's two major alliances set their war machines in motion. A flurry of diplomatic attempts over the next few days failed to halt the wheels of war from rolling forward.

Russia ordered full mobilization to begin on July 31. Austria-Hungary followed within hours. Italy declared itself neutral. To the Germans, mobilization meant war. (The lessons of the Franco-Prussian War had not been lost on them.) Germany fired off an ultimatum to Russia demanding the cessation of Russian mobilization. Russia refused.

On August 1, Germany declared war on Russia and began a general mobilization. France commenced mobilizing that same day. The next day, Germany sent an ultimatum to Belgium demanding right of passage across Belgian territory. On August 3, Germany declared war on France, and German troops began crossing the Belgian border. Belgium immediately called on Great Britain to come to its aid in defense of a treaty guaranteeing Belgium as an "independent and perpetually neutral state." The treaty had been signed in 1839 by England, France, Russia, Prussia, and Austria.

Early on August 4, Britain dispatched a communiqué to Berlin demanding that the Treaty of 1839 be upheld. The dispatch astonished German chancellor Theobold von Bethmann-Hollweg. He refused to uphold the treaty. "How," he demanded of the British ambassador, "could Britain go to war over a scrap of paper?" It was a question of honor. Britain declared war on Germany that evening.

British Foreign Secretary Sir Edward Grey, dismayed over the failure of diplomacy to curb an outbreak of international violence, viewed the rapid-fire chain of events with ominous foreboding. While standing at the window of his Whitehall office with a friend, watching as the street lamps of London were being lit below, he commented, "The lamps are going out all over Europe; we shall not see them lit again in our lifetime."

Old rivalries had resurfaced. New alliances had ensnared most of Europe. Nothing remained for the Great Powers to do in August 1914—except to make war.

German Emperor (Kaiser) Wilhelm II in the uniform of the "Death's head Hussars." A grandson of Queen Victoria and an admirer of Great Britain's naval and commercial strength, Wilhelm drifted into the First World War through a combination of arrogance, folly, and muddled thinking.

The Opposing Forces: The Men and Means for Making War

At the outbreak of World War I, the Allied armies of France, Russia, and Great Britain totaled about 2.52 million men. The combined armies of Germany and Austria-Hungary numbered roughly 1.24 million men. Mobilization rapidly ballooned these numbers to a wartime footing of some 5.36 million and 3.49 million men, respectively. These figures reflect an Allied manpower advantage of about three men to two. Numbers often mislead, however. When other factors are considered—particularly the ratio of officers, noncommissioned officers, and armaments to men—the apparent Allied advantage shrinks to a level of near-parity. Germany, in fact, held an advantage in the early months.

"Germany's opening advantage was in the fitness of her troops, the greater realism and vigor of her training methods; and a heavier, better balanced armament," writes military historian S. L. A. Marshall. "Also, the German general staff had a clearer grasp of the impact of new weapons, especially the machine gun, upon battlefield movement."

The German Empire, formed in 1871, comprised a confederation of 26 states, namely, the kingdoms of Prussia, Bavaria, Saxony, and Württemberg, plus six grand duchies, five duchies, seven principalities, three free cities (city-states), and the "imperial territory" of Alsace-Lorraine (ceded by France to Germany in 1871). Of these, Prussia—with 40 million of the Empire's population of 65 million, and under whose influence and control the Empire was formed—was the most important. Although numerous sovereigns ruled over the various states (kings, grand dukes, dukes, and princes), Wilhelm II, the Hohenzollern king of Prussia and German emperor (kaiser), ruled supremely over the German Empire.

History has characterized Wilhelm II as a vain, arrogant man, subject to mercurial mood swings. Born with a shrunken arm (because of a midwife's error), he compensated for his defect with belligerent talk and a fascination for the military and its uniforms and regalia. (Wearing a uniform also helped him to conceal his withered arm.) He spent much of his life trying to emulate his ancestor Frederick the Great, Prussian emperor-hero of the mid-18th century. Obsessed with power, Kaiser Wilhelm wielded it with trivial regard to clear thinking or to the consequences of ill-conceived decisions. He dreamed of making Germany respected, admired, and feared. But through his vacillating leadership, his inept choice of advisers, and his fondness for the military, he virtually turned over the government—and with it the prosecution of the war—to the army's high command.

Beginning in August 1914, the Kaiser spent most of his time at the *Oberste Heeresleitung* (O.H.L.), the German general headquarters, but mostly as a figurehead. He rarely interfered with his generals, who ran the war with little direction from him. At the start of the war, responsibility for planning and executing the army's strategy resided with General Count Helmuth von Moltke (the Younger), chief of the German general staff. Intelligent and thoughtful, he was a brilliant staff officer. But living in the shadow of his uncle's sterling military reputation and achievements had eroded his self-confidence. He felt far less natural affinity for war than had Moltke the Elder. To the younger Moltke, the war meant "the mutual tearing to pieces by Europe's civilized nations" and the "destruction [of] civilization in almost all Europe for decades to come."

Moltke clearly felt misgivings about the effects of war. He also felt uncomfortable with the Schlieffen Plan, Germany's master plan of attack. Count Alfred von Schlieffen, chief of the German general staff from 1891 to 1905, had developed the plan over 12 years. He completed it just before his retirement—and replacement by Moltke—in 1905. Schlieffen designed his plan to avoid a costly two-front war. Anticipating that it would take Russia about six weeks to mobilize, he planned a holding action against them in the East using minimal German forces. At the same time, the bulk of Germany's forces were to bypass France's heavily fortified eastern frontier, sweep across Luxembourg, Belgium, and northern France, and descend upon Paris in a wide arc from the north and west.

In 1905, Schlieffen captured the essence of his plan

in what came to be known as the Great Memorandum:

> If possible, the German army will win its battle by an envelopment with the right wing. This will therefore be made as strong as possible. For this purpose eight army corps and five cavalry divisions will cross the Meuse by five routes below Liège and advance in the direction of Brussels-Namur; a ninth army corps . . . will join them after crossing the Meuse above Liège. The last must also neutralize the citadel of Huy within whose range it is obliged to cross the Meuse.

In sum, assuming the success of the Schlieffen Plan, the Germans would encircle and occupy Paris and defeat France within six weeks, after which they would turn the full weight of their armies and resources against Russia in the East. But plans often go awry. Moreover, France had developed its own war plan, as had Russia and Austria-Hungary.

France's Plan 17 (XVII), developed by General Joseph J. C. Joffre, chief of the French general staff, contained no subtleties. It cut right to the action. In a word, its motif was *attack!* Joffre, whose paunchy, grandfatherly appearance belied his strength of character and bold determination, embraced *"élan,"* which roughly means that indefinable spirit that enables men to fight and carry the battle to the enemy no matter what the odds or circumstances. And he championed the French school of attack—or *offensive à outrance* (offensive to the utmost)— tersely articulated by French military theorist Lieutenant Colonel Louis Louzeau de Grandmaison: "For the attack only two things are necessary: to know where the enemy is and to decide what to do. What the enemy intends to do is of no consequence." Plan 17 relied on *élan* and featured *offensive à outrance.*

Joffre and his staff at the French General Headquarters

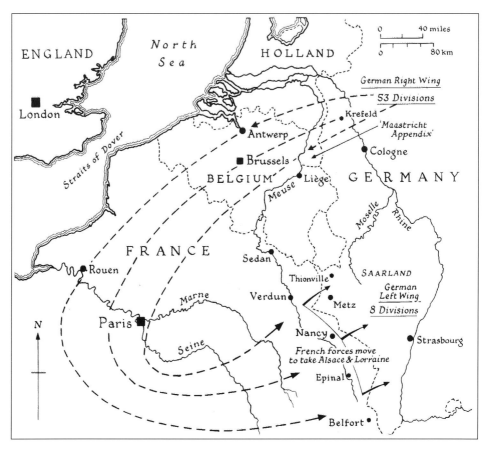

The map shows the Schlieffen Plan, intended to conquer France in six weeks' time. German armies would cross the Rhine into Belgium and invade northwest France. The plan was to seize Paris and then trap the offensive French forces, poised at Nancy, Epinal, and Verdun.

(*Grand Quartier Général*, or G.Q.G.) expected that the main thrust of a German attack would originate in the Alsace-Lorraine and strike through northeastern France. Accordingly, Plan 17 called for an immediate assault on Lorraine. In a directive sent to top-level French commanders, the G.Q.G. staff stressed the attack theme in its opening sentence: "Whatever the circumstance, it is the commander in chief's [Joffre's] intention to advance with all forces united to the attack of the German armies."

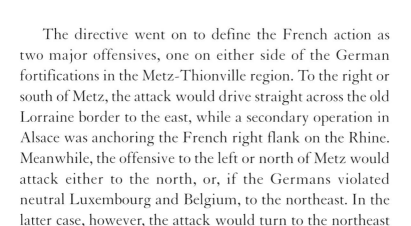

The directive went on to define the French action as two major offensives, one on either side of the German fortifications in the Metz-Thionville region. To the right or south of Metz, the attack would drive straight across the old Lorraine border to the east, while a secondary operation in Alsace was anchoring the French right flank on the Rhine. Meanwhile, the offensive to the left or north of Metz would attack either to the north, or, if the Germans violated neutral Luxembourg and Belgium, to the northeast. In the latter case, however, the attack would turn to the northeast "only by order of the commander in chief."

Critics of Plan 17 say that Joffre placed too much reliance on the Russian army's ability to mount a coordinated offensive in the East. The Russian war plan called for simultaneous offensives against both Germany and Austria-Hungary but ignored the fact that Russian mobilization would take three months. French pressure on the Russians to attack before they were ready would result in a disastrous Russian defeat in East Prussia. Despite their unreadiness, the Russians would garner some success in Galicia because of greater Austrian ineptitude in executing its overly ambitious Plan R, which also called for twin offensives (these to be mounted simultaneously against Serbia and Galicia).

Joffre also gambled—successfully—that Italy would abandon the Triple Alliance, thus his plan provided no contingency for Italian aggression. Above all, however, he and the G.Q.G. staff grossly underestimated the troop strength immediately available to the Germans. "[T]he German army presented an impressive sight upon mobilization in 1914," asserts military historian Robert B. Asprey. "Incomparably the best trained and equipped force in Europe, seven of its eight field armies or about 1,600,000 men were deployed on the western front."

A German army might vary in size from a minimum two infantry corps of nearly 90,000 to as many as seven corps

Count Helmuth Moltke was the nephew of the German strategist who had won the Franco-Prussian War. Count Moltke shared his uncle's brilliance, but lacked his assertion and willpower. Moltke altered aspects of the Schlieffen Plan, increasing the likelihood that its timetable would be upset.

plus auxiliary troops (such as Kluck's First Army that initially numbered more than 300,000 men). Each active corps comprised some 40,000 troops—two infantry divisions reinforced by such corps troops as light infantry (called *Jäger*), cavalry, heavy artillery, signal, medical, engineer, and supply. These were augmented by combat trains and an air detachment of 12 planes (for observation). Germany also activated 14 reserve corps, sufficiently trained to deploy alongside active corps but without artillery or aircraft components.

An active German infantry division numbered 17,500 men, including two infantry and one artillery brigades, plus small units—typically companies—of engineers and medical and communications personnel. Artillery consisted of 54 77-mm guns and 18 105-mm howitzers. (Guns fired high-velocity rounds at a low trajectory, whereas howitzers lobbed heavier shells at a higher trajectory.) Corps artillery supplemented these with additional 105s plus 150-mm howitzers. German field commanders could also call on 210-mm and 420-mm mortars.

The typical German rifleman or *Jäger* (literally, "hunter") carried an 1898 Mauser clip-fed, bolt-action rifle, wore a field-gray *(Feldgrau)* uniform with the famous spiked helmet *(Pickelhaube),* and bore a waterproof cowhide pack. The small infantry unit was highly disciplined and aggressively trained. Supported by the 1908 water-cooled Maxim machine gun in both offensive and defensive situations, the German rifleman represented a formidable foe.

In addition to 22 active and 14 reserve infantry corps, the Germans also fielded four cavalry corps totaling 10 divisions. A division of 7,000 men was broken into three cavalry brigades and three light-infantry *(Jäger)* battalions, plus supporting elements. Each brigade included a mounted machine-gun section of six guns and two batteries of six 77-mm guns of horse artillery.

Overall, the German soldier was well trained and perhaps better equipped than his French and British counterparts. And he enjoyed the support of more machine guns and artillery. He also had plenty of spirit, as indicated by this excerpt from the 1912 edition of the Great general staff handbook: "The general spirit of the German army is one of intense devotion to Emperor and Fatherland, combined with the conviction that no other army in the world could stand up to them for any length of time." Notwithstanding such claims, the soldiers of Britain and France held strong convictions of their own.

On August 20, 1914, German divisions entered Brussels, Belgium. Crowds gathered to watch the Germans, who were starting to be known as "Huns," after the earlier vandals led by Attila.

By August of 1914, France had mobilized five field armies plus reserve divisions and artillery groups numbering about 1.65 million men. The British Expeditionary Force, commanded by the cautious, cantankerous Sir John French, added two infantry corps and a cavalry division totaling 100,000 troops. In the early months, the B.E.F. consisted of all volunteer professional soldiers, the only army of a major European power so formed. But a great casualty toll forced Britain to resort to a draft for replacements. Although Belgium mobilized an army of 175,000 troops, it was poorly

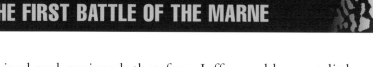

trained and equipped; therefore, Joffre could expect little help from it.

Each of France's 21 active infantry corps numbered 40,000 men. Similar in structure to the German corps, the French corps lacked heavy artillery but carried more field guns. A reserve brigade of two infantry regiments formed a part of each French corps group. Unlike the Germans, however, the French did not integrate their 25 reserve divisions into their field armies. And they preferred at first to use their 10 cavalry divisions independently rather than wed them to a corps.

In terms of weaponry, the French active division of about 15,000 troops nearly equaled the German in machine-gun strength but fell far short in heavy artillery. By contrast, the 18,000 troops of the British division matched the enemy in the number of both machine guns and heavy artillery pieces. Though pathetically outgunned in heavy artillery, the French ruled the roost in field guns. Neither the German 77-mm gun nor the British 13-pounder came close in numbers or performance to the French 75-mm gun. (Artillery was categorized either by bore diameter or weight of shell.) But the effectiveness of the French 75 was limited.

"Their [75-mm] gun was the finest quick-firing light field piece on earth," writes S. L. A. Marshall. "But its shell could do little more than batter and slow infantry moving in the open. Its blast was not sufficient to break down even nonreinforced earthworks."

The French infantryman—generally referred to as *poilu* ("hairy one")—wore red trousers and a blue jacket-cloak called a *capote* (cape). Armed with a bolt-action 1886 Lebel rifle, the *poilu,* unlike the German, marched with fixed bayonet, a lethal-looking, thin, triangular shaft of needle steel. He was always ready to launch a bayonet attack— the favorite order of his officer—at a moment's notice, even

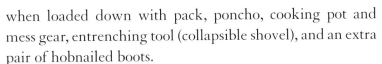

when loaded down with pack, poncho, cooking pot and mess gear, entrenching tool (collapsible shovel), and an extra pair of hobnailed boots.

Characteristically, the British soldier, or "Tommy" as he is called, a product of the Boer War in South Africa (1899-1902), represented a cross between the German and the Frenchman. He wore a light khaki uniform and was well trained for offensive and defensive warfare. To a fair degree, he understood the importance of rapid, accurate rifle fire, of advance by fire and maneuver, and of cover and concealment. The Tommy implemented the basic skills of a rifleman using the superb, although heavy, Lee-Enfield clip-fed, bolt-action rifle.

The highly trained British cavalryman also used a rifle (as opposed to the lighter but less effective carbines of other cavalry) and prided himself on his marksmanship and ability to fight either mounted or dismounted. Moreover, the B.E.F.'s massive cavalry division—five brigades totaling 14,000 men (under Allenby)—drew support from its own machine guns and horse artillery. By contrast, the French cavalryman, armed with a lance and an obsolete 1892 Lebel carbine, was ill equipped to fight on foot. But he was not less imbued with the fighting spirit of *élan*.

In midsummer of 1914, after years of planning and preparing, both the Allies and the Central Powers stood poised with the men and means for making war. On August 2 of that year, Germany delivered a 12-hour ultimatum to Belgium, demanding free passage through it. Belgium refused, pointing out that the Treaty of 1839 (guaranteeing its neutrality) was still in force. "Were the Belgian government to accept the propositions conveyed to it," Brussels informed Berlin, "it would be sacrificing the nation's honour and betraying its engagements to Europe."

Two days later, German troops invaded Belgium—and the test by fire of men and means began.

The Opening Battles: Liège, Namur, and the Frontiers of France

During the last days of August, strange scenes such as this one were common in Belgium and northern France. Soldiers dug trenches while peasants reaped grain.

On August 4, 1914, a specially trained task force from Major General Karl von Bülow's German Second Army crossed the Belgian frontier between the Ardennes and the Dutch border. Led by General Otto von Emmich, the task force of about 30,000 men advanced down the narrow corridor of Belgian territory between Holland and Luxembourg toward Liège, one of the most heavily defended cities in Europe.

The forts at both Liège and Namur guarded the Meuse River crossings. Designed by Belgian military engineer General Henri Brialmont and built between 1888 and 1892, they represented the most modern fortresses in Europe. The fortifications of each city consisted of 12 forts that encircled the city in a 25-mile circumference, positioned to defend the city itself, as well as to provide protective fire for one another. Built of armor-plated concrete to withstand assault by the heaviest gun then exist-ing—the 210-mm (8.4-in)—the fortress cities stood squarely in the path of the German invaders and had to be sur-mounted. The plan was to overtake Liège first, then Namur. In keeping with its timetable, the German high command allotted Emmich's task force 48 hours to topple the city.

The Germans had anticipated no resistance by the Belgians; or, at worst, an easily overcome token show of force. But they had not figured on the determination of Belgian monarch Albert I to defend his nation's territory. Albert immediately issued orders to destroy the bridges over the Meuse at Liège, along with the railway bridges and tunnels at the Luxembourg border. He further directed General Gérard Mathieu Leman, commander of the fortified complex at Liège, "to hold to the end."

Meanwhile, before a shot was fired at Liège, Kaiser Wilhelm II, hoping in one last desperate move to dissuade Britain from joining the war, asked General von Moltke if he could quickly shift his armies to the east. The kaiser hoped to give the appearance of girding for a one-front war. Moltke rightly responded that such a move in quick time was impos-sible. Wilhelm replied, "Your uncle would have given me a different answer." The kaiser's words hurt Moltke deeply.

Moltke later wrote: "I felt as if my heart would break . . . when I got home I was like a broken man, and shed tears of despair." The Kaiser abandoned his abrupt change of think-ing and the near-crisis passed. But the 66-year-old chief of the German general staff could not "get over this experience. It was as though something in me had been irretrievably shaken. My confidence and self-reliance were destroyed." Such was the top German commander's frame of mind when the invasion of Belgium—and World War I—commenced.

Upon crossing the border, advance elements of Emmich's contingent distributed leaflets disclaiming aggressive intent but soon met resistance from Belgian cavalrymen and cyclist troops. That night, *franc-tireurs*, or "free-shooters" (snipers), acting in what they considered to be the legitimate defense of their neutral territory, harassed the invaders in cities and towns already occupied. The Germans, claiming that the Belgians were illegally using civilians to harass them, sought collective retribution in the town of Hervé. Five days later, a German journalist following behind the invaders found Hervé "razed to the ground." Of some 500 houses in the town, he reported, "only 19 remain. Corpses are lying all over the place; everywhere there is a smell of burning. The church is a broken heap of ruins."

On August 5, when word of Hervé's tragic fate reached Moltke, he wrote, "Our advance in Belgium is certainly brutal, but we are fighting for our lives and all who get in the way must take the consequences." The "consequences" were to worsen over the next three weeks, which saw the invaders slaughter innocent civilians—including women and children—in village after village: at Andenne, 211 dead; at Tamines, 384; at Dinant, 612; and on it went.

When Emmich and his forces reached Liège on August 5, they found that the bridges above and below the city had been blown up. Two bridges leading into the city itself remained standing but were almost impossible to cross under heavy defensive fire. Emmich sent an emissary into the city demanding Leman's surrender. The crusty Belgian commander sent the emissary off in a huff. Emmich responded with an artillery bombardment, followed by a night infantry attack that lasted into the next day and cost him such severe casualties that he had to call on Bülow for reinforcements.

On August 7, General Erich Ludendorf, liaison officer between Bülow's Second Army and Emmich's task force, assumed command of the German Fourteenth Brigade after the death of its commander while in action. With uncommon courage and daring, Ludendorf led a group of 1,500 men through the outer ring of forts at Liège and seized the city, only to find that Leman and his defenders had taken refuge in Fort Loncin on the west side of the outer ring. Ludendorf now held the city but was surrounded by Belgians with insufficient strength to force their surrender. And most of Emmich's forces remained outside the ring.

With the Belgians still holding firm at the Meuse crossings so vital to the German advance and to the success of the Schlieffen Plan, Ludendorf persuaded Bülow to bring forward the new, first road-transportable Krupp 420-mm (16.5-in) heavy howitzer—soon to become famous as the *Dicke Berta,* or "Big Bertha." It arrived within range of the outer ring on August 12, the same day that the first British troops crossed the English Channel. The huge howitzer— joined by a second Big Bertha the next day—commenced the systematic dismantling of the Belgian forts, "stripping away armour plate and blocks of concrete, cracking arches and poisoning the air with heavy brown fumes."

The forts fell one by one to the big guns of Krupp and smaller siege guns: first, Fort Pontisse, then Forts Embourg, Chaudfontaine, Liers, Fléron, Boncelle, and Lautin. German guns then turned on Fort Loncin on August 15. After a 140-minute bombardment, Loncin's munitions magazine blew up and leveled the fortress. The remaining forts—Flémalle, Hollogne, Barchon, and Mevegnée— surrendered the next day. Albert I pulled back his troops in defense of Antwerp. Kluck's German First Army and Bülow's Second poured through the Liège corridor. Brussels fell to the Germans on August 20. Emmich moved his guns to Namur and repeated his crushing victory of Liège after three days of bombardment on August 24. Antwerp held out stubbornly against the Germans but would finally fall on October 9.

King Albert of Belgium with General Otto von Emmich. Germany had expected Belgium to allow German troops to pass through peacefully, but King Albert and his people resisted valiantly.

Some say that the heroic Belgian stand at Liège delayed the German timetable, but not Ludendorf. "We got possession of all the works just in time to permit the march of the army over the Meuse without hindrance," he said. Moreover, history shows that more than 1 million German soldiers had crossed the Rhine and arrived in the forward zone by August 12—the day that the first elements of Sir John French's B.E.F. debarked in France and advanced toward Mons. Two days later, the German and Anglo-French forces clashed in what historians now call the Frontiers of France (or Battles of the Frontiers).

In the meantime, on August 4, General Joseph J. C. Joffre, Allied commander in chief and chief of the French general staff, had moved his staff headquarters (G.Q.G.) to Vitry-le-François on the Marne. This field location, about halfway between Paris and Nancy, positioned him within 80 to 90 miles of each of his five army headquarters. Four days later, Joffre set the forces of Plan 17 in motion. General Paul Pau's army of Alsace, anchoring the French right flank, advanced to Mulhouse in Alsace.

Joffre then launched a full-scale offensive south of Metz, sending his First and Second Armies, under Generals Auguste Dubail and Noël de Castelnau, respectively, driving into Lorraine. In the ensuing fighting—later dubbed the Battle of Lorraine (August 14 to 22)—the German Sixth Army under Crown Prince Rupprecht of Bavaria and the Seventh led by General Josias von Heeringen backed off quickly in a planned withdrawal. Suddenly and unexpectedly, however, the two German armies turned about on their attackers and mounted a converging counterattack, throwing back the Frenchmen to the fortified heights of Nancy.

With the French Second Army in full retreat, Castelnau's XX Corps arrived at Nancy. Commanded by General Ferdinand Foch, a brilliant officer destined for future greatness, XX Corps played a decisive role in Nancy's defense. Foch later recalled, "On the 21st we had to continue the withdrawal. . . . I went to Nancy. They wanted to evacuate it. I said: 'The enemy is two days' march distant from Nancy and XX Corps is there. They won't walk over the XX without protest!'" And they did not. His corps

The Krupp arms works in Germany produced many new and powerful war weapons. One of the best known was "Big Bertha," a howitzer, which had a range of 122 kilometers (75.8 miles).

took the offensive and helped to extend France's border back to the east bank of the Rhine.

Meanwhile, to the north of Metz, the advancing French Third and Fourth Armies, respectively led by Generals Pierre Ruffey and Fernand de Langle de Cary, ran headlong into the German Fourth and Fifth Armies commanded, in order, by Duke Albrecht of Württemberg and Crown Prince Wilhelm. The two German armies formed the pivot of the Schlieffen Plan movement. In four days of furious fighting known as the Battle of the Ardennes (August 20-25), the Germans inflicted huge losses on the outnumbered French armies and drove them back to the west of the Meuse. Ruffey and Langle de Cary dug in and regrouped their forces with the French right flank anchored at the fortress of Verdun.

"The French showed ardor and nothing else," comments military historian S. L. A. Marshall. "They did not try to advance in short rushes or to wiggle forward or to make a stealthy use of ground in their approaches. Their battle kits contained no grenades. They charged straight in, expecting by audacity to stampede the enemy. By today's view, that is madness." But such audacity, of course, exemplified *élan*.

While the fighting raged in the Ardennes, the "wheel" of the Schlieffen maneuver, represented by the German First, Second, and Third Armies in the northwest, led by Generals Kluck, Bülow, and Max Klemens von Hausen, respectively, began "wheeling" west and southwest. In the Battle of the Sambre, or Charleroi (August 22-23), Joffre, in accordance with the contingency provisions of Plan 17, sent General Charles Lanrezac's French Fifth Army into the angle formed by the nexus of the Meuse and Sambre Rivers to counter the German maneuver.

In the Meuse-Sambre angle, Lanrezac faced Hausen's Third Army to the northeast and the approach of Bülow's Second Army to the northwest. Bülow, leaving Emmich to besiege Namur, had crossed the Sambre in two places between Namur and Charleroi with most of his army, capturing Charleroi on August 21. Lanrezac's courageous *poilus* fought fiercely but were unable to check the German advance. Bayonet charge after charge into withering machine-gun fire canceled out thousands of young French lives in the name of *élan,* until Lanrezac wisely ordered a general retreat on August 23. Unfortunately, amid the frenzied fighting, Lanrezac neglected to send word of his withdrawal to the British on his left flank.

Sir John French's British expeditionary forces had arrived at Mons and deployed along the Mons-Condé Canal in Belgium on August 22. The next day, while Lanrezac's army began pulling back, the British Tommies fought furiously to hold off the sweep of Kluck's German First Army as it began its scythe-like movement to the west. The British fought all day with no knowledge of their exposed right flank and no troops to their left.

That evening, when Sir John learned of Lanrezac's retirement, he ordered his own troops to withdraw in the morning. The Battle of Mons, which had appeared at first to be a great British victory, became equally well known as the British Retreat from Mons. In a later comment about Lanrezac' pullback, Winston Churchill, then lord of the admiralty, wrote, "[I]t was a pity he forgot to tell his British allies about it."

The roughly nine-day period of fighting along the frontiers of France ended in a catastrophic defeat for France and its British ally, leaving the northern frontier breached at every point of German attack. Moltke, over-estimating his victories, sent reinforcements originally intended for his right-flank armies to bolster his new offensive in Lorraine. He also detached two corps from his right flank and sent them to the eastern front to quell an unexpected Russian initiative. Both actions diluted the original Schlieffen Plan, whose originator had reportedly said with his dying words, "Keep the right flank strong."

If Schlieffen's plan suffered some degradation, Joffre's Plan 17 failed miserably, costing 300,000 casualties among the 1.25 million French troops who participated in the fighting. German casualties equaled those of the French. British losses totaled 4,244. Considering its brief time span, the number of troops involved, and the rate and number of casualties on both sides, the Frontiers of France marked the greatest battle of World War I. And it ensured that the war would be fought in France—beginning at Le Câteau and Guise.

The Great Retreat: Germans at the Gate

British General Haig inspecting French troops in Paris. Throughout the war there was tension between British and French commanders, because their nations had so often fought each other in the past. Communications at the infantry level were better, but difficult because few British spoke French, and vice-versa.

In their Retreat from Mons, starting on August 24, 1914, the British joined in the general withdrawal of French forces all along the front, from Mons to Mulhouse. This massive Allied retirement became known as the Great Retreat. On that same day, General Joffre sent a message to French Minister of War Adolphe Messimy explaining the necessity for pulling back the entire front:

> Our army corps . . . have not shown on the battlefield those offensive qualities for which we had hoped . . . . We are therefore compelled to resort to the defensive, using our fortresses and great topographical obstacles to enable us to yield as little ground as possible. Our object must be to last out, trying to wear the enemy down, and to resume the offensive when the time comes.

The Allied commander in chief's message went on to lay out a rough recovery plan aimed at resuming the initiative and seizing victory from imminent defeat. Over the next two weeks, the Great Retreat—despite a series of delaying actions—would carry the Anglo-French armies back to the outskirts of Paris, while the unflappable Joffre worked calmly to smooth the rough edges off his plan for an incredible reversal of fortune.

The enveloping maneuver of Kluck's First Army on the German right flank had at last become clear, and the original mission of the B.E.F. to reinforce Joffre's left flank took on even greater criticality. To aid the B.E.F., Joffre hurriedly sent General J. F. A. Sordet's French cavalry corps and a garrison division from the recently declared open city of Lille to bolster three territorial divisions already filling the void between the B.E.F. and the sea. Joffre's plan-in-progress called for the B.E.F. to hold the space between Lanrezac's Fifth Army and the newly forming Sixth Army, while withdrawing at a pace in consort with the pace of the general retreat. Joffre further intended for the British to hold fast once they reached St.-Quentin on the Somme. Field Marshal Sir John French had a different idea.

With four German corps advancing against him, with Lanrezac's Fifth Army in full retreat to his now exposed right, and with the whole French offensive collapsing, Sir John's first thought was to save the B.E.F. from total annihilation. He ordered his troops to retreat at once to Le Câteau and moved his headquarters 26 miles farther back to St.-Quentin. In a fighting withdrawal, General Sir Horace L. Smith-Dorrien's II Corps did most of the fighting.

First, after a delay in the order to retreat, a battalion of Cheshires, Fifteenth Brigade, failed to get the word and found itself surrounded by Germans at Andrecies. When the Cheshires finally fought through the circle of foes, only two officers and 200 men out of an original 1,000 survived to talk about it.

Then, near Elouges, a second German attack struck the Fifteenth Brigade in flank and claimed another 1,100 casualties. By nightfall of the 24th, Smith-Dorrien had lost 3,800 men, or about 17 percent of his fighting strength. In typical British understatement, the official B.E.F. history described the engagement as "the flank guard action at Elouges." Smith-Dorrien's only solace on the day came when the Fourth Division and the Nineteenth Brigade arrived from England to reinforce II Corps.

The next day, General Sir Douglas Haig's I Corps and Smith-Dorrien's II Corps split apart on either side of the forest of Mormal, 10 miles long and 6 miles wide. Haig's corps, on the B.E.F.'s right flank (facing the enemy), fell back along the roads across the Sambre, while Smith-Dorrien and General Edmund H. H. Allenby's cavalry dropped straight back on the left. I Corps, failing to notice that the forest contained passable roads through it, fell victim to an enemy surprise attack at Landrecies where they had planned on camping for the night.

Upon entering the town, Haig's men encountered a body of troops wearing French uniforms, whose officer responded to a British challenge in French. Suddenly, according to Brigadier General James E. Edmonds, the official British historian, the French-uniformed troops "without the slightest warning lowered their bayonets and charged." The ostensibly friendly troops turned out to be elements of Kluck's IV Corps, who also had planned on bedding down for the night in Landrecies.

In the ensuing skirmish, involving about two regiments and a gun battery on each side, the stress and uncertainty of night action led Haig to believe that his corps had fallen under heavy attack. At 10:00 P.M., he telephoned G.H.Q. requesting help and emphasizing, "Situation very critical." Fearing Haig's envelopment—or worse, a German penetration between I and

British and Belgian troops retreat from Mons. The Allied retreat
opened the way for the continuation of the Schlieffen Plan.

II Corps—B.E.F. commander Sir John French called on
Smith-Dorrien to rush help to Haig, in the form of, if nothing
more, the newly arrived Nineteenth Corps. Sir John also
instructed Haig to alter his line of retreat for the next day.

Sir John's order to Haig set I Corps on a line of march on
the opposite side of the Oise River from Smith Dorrien's II
Corps. This effectively severed direct contact between the two
corps for the next seven days. Moreover, Sir John's plea to
Smith-Dorrien could not have found him less able to lend
assistance to Haig. Roads clogged with fleeing refugees and
sharp fighting in several locations had slowed his withdrawal.
By nightfall on the 25th, Smith-Dorrien's corps, dog tired

from three days of fighting and marching under a hot summer sun, stood scattered on a line stretching from Solesmes to Le Câteau. Smith-Dorrien did not send the Nineteenth Brigade to Haig. At that moment, Smith-Dorrien did not even know where it was. But he knew that the enemy had almost caught up to him.

On August 26 at 2:00 A.M., General Allenby rode in to II Corps H.Q. and warned Smith-Dorrien that the Germans were positioned for an attack at dawn. Allenby advised him to move his troops "*at once* and get away *in the dark*" or face a crushing attack by powerful German forces at first light. With II Corps spread across the countryside, and with some elements still arriving in Le Câteau, Smith-Dorrien knew that he could not possibly reach all of his units in time to call for an immediate withdrawal. Nor could he expect his exhausted troops to march any farther without some rest. He had no telephone contact with G.H.Q., so the decision to move or fight resided with him alone.

Smith-Dorrien asked Allenby if he would accept orders from him. Allenby said yes. "Very well, gentlemen, we will fight," Smith-Dorrien declared, in one of the most controversial decisions of the Marne campaign. He added that he would also ask the Fourth Division and Nineteenth Brigade commanders if they would join the battle. They would. Given the circumstances, the Battle of Le Câteau was unavoidable. It began at daybreak.

Kluck attacked with a rage born of frustration. He had failed for two days to drive the B.E.F.—which he considered defeated—back to Maubeuge, about 50 miles southeast of Lille on the Sambre. The artillery of five German divisions opened up on the British at dawn, answered all along the line by British 18-pounder and powerful 60-pounder guns. In shallow trenches and from behind stone walls, British sharpshooters repulsed wave upon wave of German attackers. When surrounded by Germans in one sector, a company of Argylls kept firing their Short Magazine Lee-Enfields "bringing down man after man and counting their scores aloud," while the Germans "kept sounding the British 'Cease Fire' and gesturing to persuade the men to surrender but in vain." The Germans eventually rushed and overwhelmed the Argylls.

While the artillery duel thundered all morning, Kluck's left corps worked through Le Câteau and nearby villages and advanced across rolling hills partitioned by bramble hedgerows to arrive at Smith-Dorrien's right flank. It now stood exposed and vulnerable because Haig had disengaged from his lesser action at Landrecies and resumed his retreat to the south. Fergusson's Fifth Division held the right flank, with its own right guarded by the Nineteenth Brigade. They fought with rare fury and suffered frightful losses. Fergusson lost most of his guns and many of his small units. If things were bad on Smith-Dorrien's right, they were worse on his left.

The Fourth Division under General Snow had joined the battle lacking cavalry, communications, field ambulances, engineers, and—most critical—artillery, and had arrived in a state of general disorder. One of its young officers, Lieutenant Bernard L. Montgomery, who in another time and place would command great armies, remembered being deployed in a forward company, when

> The C.O. [commanding officer] galloped up to us forward companies and shouted to us to attack the enemy on the forward hill at once. This was the only order; there was no reconnaissance, no plan, no covering fire. We rushed up the hill, came under heavy fire, my Company Commander was wounded and there were many casualties. Nobody knew what to do, so we returned to the original position from which we had begun to attack. If this was real war it struck me as most curious.

Real war, Montgomery was learning, is as curious as it is tragic. Had it not been for the heroics of Sordet's cavalry and

Bernard Montgomery was a British infantry captain in 1914.
Twenty-eight years later he led the British to their victory over
Rommel at El-Alamein in North Africa.

the Eighty-Fourth French Territorial Division briefly
holding off Kluck's advance on Smith-Dorrien's left, the
B.E.F. might have been enveloped and obliterated. As it was,
Smith-Dorrien, with both his right and left flanks collapsing
by midafternoon, ordered a general disengagement and
retirement at 5:00 P.M.

By some near-miracle, the exhausted commanders of II

Corps spread the word to their equally spent troops, formed rear guards, and gradually broke off action along the line. The word to retreat never reached some units, such as the Gordon Highlanders, who stayed behind and fought until they ceased to exist. By dark, however, the first columns of Smith-Dorrien's command began slogging toward Reumont, 16 miles to the south. A cold, heavy rain joined them on the march—a fitting end to a rotten day at Le Câteau.

The British official history characterizes the day's events in a rather more upbeat tenor: "[T]he whole of Smith-Dorrien's troops had done what was thought to be impossible. With both flanks more or less in the air, they had turned upon an enemy of at least twice their strength; had struck him hard, and had withdrawn . . . practically without interference." In conclusion, the official history notes, "The men looked upon themselves as victors, some indeed doubted whether they had been in a serious action."

Through German eyes, the situation appeared vastly different, as indicated by an official O.H.L. communiqué released on August 27: "The German armies have entered France from Cambrai to the Vosges after a series of continually victorious combats. The enemy, beaten all along the line, is in full retreat . . . and not capable of offering serious resistance to the German advance."

When the day ended, Smith-Dorrien's losses totaled more than 8,000 men and 38 guns—more than twice his losses at Mons, more even than Wellington's losses against Napoleon at Waterloo in 1815. After five days of fighting in France, casualties for the B.E.F. now stood at 15,000 men, or about 20 percent, approximately equivalent to the loss percentage incurred by French forces on all fronts in August.

Smith-Dorrien had succeeded in temporarily stopping three enemy corps and perhaps saving the B.E.F. from extinction—which again demonstrated the fighting qualities of the British "Tommy"—but serious problems existed within the B.E.F. Lack of coordination between I and II Corps resulted in I Corps failing to mount a flank attack on Kluck's three First Army corps in the Battle of Le Câteau. And Sir John's failure to exert control of his forces, left Smith-Dorrien to shift for himself against an enemy far superior in numbers. After the battle, Haig's relatively unscathed I Corps continued retreating away from II Corps and increasing the gap between them to 15 miles by August 28.

On August 29, Joffre ordered Lanrezac's French Fifth Army—itself already pressed hard by Major General Karl von Bülow's German Second Army—to swing 90 degrees westward and attack the left flank of Kluck's First Army in the vicinity of Guise-St.-Quentin. Joffre wanted to relieve pressure on the British. The initial attack failed in the ensuing battle—called Guise by the French, St.-Quentin by the Germans. But Lanrezac's I Corps, a reserve force led by General Louis Franchet d'Esperey on a chestnut charger, moved swiftly to the attack.

By dusk, stacks of German dead littered the bridge at Guise and the French could sense enemy resistance weakening on the far side of the Oise River. An eyewitness later reported, "The Germans were running away." And the French "frantic with joy at the new and longed for sensation were carried forward in a splendid victorious wave." Their joy subsided quickly. At 10 o'clock that night, Joffre, still very much aware of the threat posed to his left flank by Kluck's advancing First Army, ordered Lanrezac to retreat and blow up the bridges of the Oise behind him. Bülow perceived the French withdrawal as a victory for his Second Army.

The next day, August 30, Parisians could hear the distant rumble of German guns. Overhead, a Taube monoplane with Maltese crosses on its wings appeared and dropped leaflets onto the streets of Paris, proclaiming: "PEOPLE OF PARIS SURRENDER! The Germans are at your gates! You can do nothing but surrender."

General Alexander von Kluck was a typical Prussian leader, vigorous, decisive, and imbued with the glorious history of the Prussian army. Kluck made the fateful decision to turn his First Army east of Paris rather than sweep around it to the west.

Decision at Châtillon: The Battle Begins

O n August 30, the same day that leaflets of impending doom fell on Parisians, General Karl von Bülow notified O.H.L., now located in Luxembourg, of a "complete victory" at St.-Quentin. Although he had sustained 6,000 casualties in his clash with Lanrezac's Fifth Army, Bülow did not want General Alexander von Kluck's performance at Le Câteau to outstrip his own. He also signaled Kluck on his right: "Enemy decisively beaten today." That night, Bülow appealed unexpectedly to Kluck: "To gain the full advantage of victory, a wheel inward of the First Army pivoted on Chauny toward the line La Fère-Leon is urgently desired." A gap was opening between the First and Second Armies. Kluck received Bülow's request while on a line of march toward the Avre River, a

southwesterly course in accordance with Moltke the Younger's directive of August 27.

In Moltke's directive, he had updated the missions of the German armies: First Army was to advance on the lower Seine, keeping west of the Oise, while Second Army marched on Paris; Third Army was to march on Château-Thierry, Fourth Army on Epernay; Fifth Army was to envelop Verdun; and the Sixth and Seventh Armies were to stand on the defensive in Lorraine and Alsace.

Despite having weakened the right wing further yet by reassigning five additional corps to duties elsewhere on both the Western and Eastern Fronts, Moltke still called on the right wing to deliver a quick victory. But he ended his precise directive on a note of indecision. "If the enemy puts up strong resistance on the Aisne and later on the Marne," he wrote, "it may be necessary to abandon the southwestern direction of the advance and wheel south." Moltke's vacillation invited trouble.

Kluck and Bülow had already disputed the direction to be taken. Prior to entering Belgium, Moltke had assigned oversight of the right wing to Bülow for better cohesion and control. Because of Moltke's depletion of the right wing, Bülow now favored stopping any further westward extension before losing the already dwindling cohesion and control, whereas Kluck wanted to advance by whatever avenue promised the quickest reward. Moltke's directive not only provided strategic license to the field commanders, it also released Kluck from Bülow's charge. Surprisingly, Moltke's wavering brought Kluck and Bülow into partial agreement.

Kluck wired Moltke of his intention to "wheel inward"— but to the *south*east as opposed to directly *east* as requested by Bülow. (A sharp turn to his left seemed illogical to Kluck if the flank and rear of the retreating French were to be attacked.) Moltke wired back his concurrence. Kluck shifted his direction on August 31, leaving behind only General Hans von Gronau's IV Reserve Corps to protect his right flank.

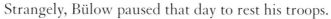

Strangely, Bülow paused that day to rest his troops.

Kluck, thinking that he had driven the British from his front, mistakenly believed that the French Fifth Army now formed the Allied left flank. Although he had engaged in a few minor clashes with French troops on his right—actually part of the assembling French Sixth Army—he had discounted them as unimportant scattered elements. Kluck felt so confident of a quick victory that he failed to report them. Instead, he ignored them and aggressively shifted his attack to roll back Lanrezac's Fifth Army. His shift in direction would cause him to pass to the east of Paris—rather than to the west—with his right flank only marginally protected. So, with the full knowledge of Moltke, Kluck scrapped the last vestiges of the Schlieffen Plan.

On September 2, Kluck's right flank stood on the Oise, near Chantilly, his left on the Marne at Château-Thierry. At this point, Moltke vacillated again. He wired Kluck that it was "the intention of the high command to drive the French back in a south-easterly direction, cutting them off from Paris. The First Army will follow the Second in echelon and will also cover the right flank of the armies."

Moltke, it seemed, now considered the destruction of the enemy's armies of more importance than the capture of Paris. He clearly lacked the necessary troop strength on his right to envelop the French capital. Moreover, with the British (ostensibly) defeated, the main enemy strength now lay in front of his center armies. If Kluck and Bülow could break through on the right and Rupprecht on the left, he could crush the enemy forces in a classic double envelopment and still bring the war to an end within six weeks.

Kluck's First Army still carried the key to the success of Moltke's ever-fluctuating strategy. But Moltke, in his amended order for Kluck to follow Bülow "in echelon" and "cover the right flank," failed to recognize that Kluck had already advanced far ahead of the slower-moving Bülow.

To comply with Moltke's latest order now, Kluck would have to halt his army for at least two days and wait for Bülow to catch up with him—time enough for the French to either slip away to the east or rally. Kluck now faced a dilemma. While Kluck pondered his problems, General Joffre was juggling a few of his own.

Joffre, on receiving news of Kluck's change of direction from British air observers and his own cavalry on August 31, wanted to return to the offensive as soon as possible with all of the forces, especially British forces, that he could muster. But Field Marshal Sir John French just wanted to return home. Sir John felt totally exasperated by the French way of waging war and feared that he might lose his entire command to French ineptitude.

In a wire to British War Minister Kitchener, Sir John hinted at his intentions: "I have decided to begin my retirement tomorrow in the morning, behind the Seine, in a southwesterly direction west of Paris. This means marching for some eight days." It really meant that Sir John was checking himself and his troops out of the war and heading for the port of St.-Nazaire, where he planned to reembark with the B.E.F. for England.

In an emergency meeting with the British prime minister and a hastily summoned Cabinet, Kitchener explained that Sir John's move "might mean nothing less than the loss of the war." Kitchener left for Paris that evening. On September 1, during a closed-door conversation, the war minister ordered Sir John back into action. Sir John obeyed.

That night, Kitchener telegraphed London with news of his successful meeting: "French's troops are now in the fighting line, where he will remain conforming to the movements of the French army." Sir John would remain for another year and a half.

That same day, after six days of continuous marching southward, Lanrezac's Fifth Army arrived in Craonne, 15 miles southeast of Laon. The recently promoted Captain Edward L. Spears, Sir John's liaison officer with the Fifth Army, described the condition of the suffering *poilus* and their horses this way:

> Heads down, red trousers and blue coats indistinguishable for dust, bumping into transport, into abandoned carts, into each other, they shuffled down the endless roads, their eyes filled with dust that dimmed the scalding landscape, so that they saw clearly only the foreground of discarded packs, prostrate men, and an occasional abandoned gun. Dead and dying horses that had dropped in their tracks from fatigue, lay in great numbers by the side of the roads. Worse still, horses dying but not yet dead, sometimes struggling a little, a strange appeal in their eyes, looked at the passing columns whose dust covered them, caking their thirsty lips and nostrils.

Joffre ordered Lanrezac's general retirement to continue until the Fifth Army was out of immediate danger of envelopment. He then turned his attention back to his plan-in-progress and to the men and means for implementing it. Joffre had begun to formulate his recovery plan on August 24, the day when the failure of Plan 17 had become clear. It was almost time to set the new plan in motion.

Joffre's recovery plan resembled the Schlieffen Plan in reverse. It would pivot about Verdun and the Nancy heights, where his First and Second Armies were to hold at all costs. Meanwhile, his Third, Fourth, and Fifth Armies and the B.E.F. would withdraw to a general line of the Somme River-Verdun.

While the southeasterly withdrawals were in progress, Joffre drew off elements from his embattled right flank and from units in the interior of France to form two new armies. The Sixth Army, under General Michel J. Maunoury, was

assembled first near Amiens and later in and around Paris. Positioned west of the German First Army, it was to attack Kluck's right flank. Of the 67-year-old, slightly built Maunoury, Joffre said, "This is a complete soldier."

The Ninth Army, under General Ferdinand Foch, would deploy behind the Fourth and Fifth Armies and supply support and additional weight for a counterattack against the main enemy effort. The counterattack was to be launched upon completion of the general withdrawal. Under Foch, the Ninth would be guided by a leader described by one military historian as "France's finest soldier of the 20th century."

On September 2, with Kluck's First Army moving toward the Marne River, the French government transferred its seat from Paris to Bordeaux. War Minister Etienne-Alexandre Millerand left the defense of the city and its gathering military forces in the hands of General Joseph-Simon Galliéni, the newly appointed military governor of Paris. Galliéni took his new duties seriously. On notices posted about the city, he proclaimed to the city's military forces and citizens:

> The members of the Government of the Republic have left Paris to give a new impulse to the national defense. I have received a mandate to defend Paris against the invader. This mandate I shall carry out to the end.

Few Parisians doubted his words. The thin, frail, 65-year-old general intended to defend his beloved city *à outrance*— to the utmost.

The next day, Joffre motored to Lanrezac's headquarters at Sézanne and told him, "My friend, you are used up and undecided. You will have to give up command of the Fifth Army." Lanrezac had frequently questioned Joffre's orders and now paid the price for it. Joffre replaced him with Franchet d'Esperey.

North of the Marne, Kluck, unable to communicate

French General Joseph Galliéni was 65 when the First World War began. Although his training and his experience came from 19th century warfare, Galliéni adapted to the situation and became one of the heroes in saving Paris from the German invasion.

with O.H.L. and unaware of the Army of Paris (the Paris garrison and Maunoury's Sixth Army, still forming to the west), tried to carry out the intent of Moltke's amended—if confused—instruction of September 2. He reasoned that Moltke wanted the French driven southeast of Paris in an enveloping movement by his ideally positioned army.

Accordingly, the pugnacious Kluck continued south and crossed the Marne, only a day behind the B.E.F. His right flank remained wide open, while trainloads of troops bound for the new French Sixth Army poured into Paris.

On the 4th, Joffre issued his attack order: "It is desirable to take advantage of the exposed position of the German First Army to concentrate against it the strength of the Allied armies [opposite]." His General Instruction Number 6 directed the Sixth Army in the west to cross the Ourcq, a tributary of the Marne, and advance around Kluck's flank. At the same time, the B.E.F. and the Fifth and Ninth Armies were to launch a fighting advance northward. Joffre established September 6 as the effective date of his order.

Meanwhile, in Luxembourg, Moltke had begun to feel uneasy about reports of an enemy troop buildup in and around Paris and foresaw a potential threat to the exposed right flank of Kluck's First Army. On September 5, Moltke issued a General Directive contravening his orders of September 2:

> The enemy has evaded the enveloping attack of the First and Second Armies, and a part of his forces has joined up with those about Paris . . . the attempt to force the whole French army back in a southeasterly direction toward the Swiss frontier is thus rendered impracticable. It is far more probable that the enemy is bringing up new formations and concentrating superior forces in the neighborhood of Paris, to protect the capital and threaten the right flank of the German army.

Moltke therefore ordered the First and Second Armies to stand on the defensive outside Paris. The Third Army was to advance toward the upper Seine, while the Fourth and Fifth Armies were attacking to the southeast. This, Moltke thought, would clear the way for the Sixth and Seventh to cross the Moselle River and complete the envelopment of the enemy.

Moltke's orders represented a reversal of the plan envisioned by Schlieffen, which called for the First and Second Armies to drive the enemy against the German left wing, not the other way around. In any case, the order meant that Kluck would have to retrace his steps and swing his front from south to west. When he received the order early on the 5th, Kluck thought that Moltke must still be confused. He sent a message to O.H.L. noting that the Paris forces were still forming and did not pose an immediate threat, whereas his vanguard had already made contact with the B.E.F. and the French Fifth Army's left. Kluck opted to continue south to his army's objective for the day. But he ordered Gronau's corps to halt where it stood near the Ourcq.

While Kluck continued south, Joffre sped off for B.E.F. headquarters in Melun to see Sir John French and guarantee the full support of the British in the battle line. At Melun, Sir John appeared "lukewarm" toward an offensive. Joffre crashed his fist down on the conference table and blurted, *"Monsieur le Maréchal* [Mister Marshal], the honor of England is at stake!"

Sir John flushed. Tears formed in his eyes and spilled over. He struggled briefly to say something in French then gave up. In English, he said to an interpreter, "Damn it, I can't explain. Tell him that all that men can do our fellows will do."

Joffre looked toward the interpreter, who said, "The field marshal says 'Yes.'"

Following a serving of tea, Joffre returned to his new headquarters at Châtillon-sur-Seine and summoned his staff on the evening of September 5. "Gentlemen," he said to his assembled officers, "we will fight on the Marne."

While Joffre had been seeking assurances of British help, elements of Maunoury's Sixth Army, while advancing toward the Ourcq to position themselves for the next day's offensive, were attacked by a German corps. And the first great battle of the war began a day early.

French soldiers use a captured German machine gun against the enemy during the First Battle of the Marne. The Germans were greatly superior in heavy artillery; the French had the advantage in light field guns.

Moments of Glory: Deciding the Fate of France

The Marne, the river from which the first great battle of World War I drew its name, begins in northeast central France. It flows northwest and west for 326 miles and joins the Seine near Paris at Charenton-le-Pont. Its deep trench forms the most formidable natural barrier in the region of Île-de-France. Its main tributaries—the Ourcq, the Petit Morin, and the Grand Morin—are also deeply guttered. The Ourcq flows north to south, across the line of Maunoury's advance; and the Morins flow east to west, and thus across the front of the B.E.F. and the French Fifth and Ninth Armies. To the right of the Ninth, further impeding its movements, lay the Marshes of St.-Gond, a near-impenetrable east-west belt that forms a part of the riverine system. None of these waterways presented an insurmountable barrier, but they defined the battle-field and channeled the action, beginning at the Ourcq.

Early on September 5, General Michel Maunoury's Sixth Army, under the overall command of General Joseph-Simon Galliéni, the military governor of Paris, started moving toward the inviting right flank of General Alexander von Kluck's First Army. Maunoury's forces, still not completely organized, comprised two regular and two reserve divisions, a brigade of black Moroccans, a cavalry brigade, and an Algerian division.

At about 11:00 that same morning, General Hans von Gronau's IV Reserve Corps reached his day's objective near Barcy, west of the Ourcq River. His understaffed corps, depleted by transfers to other units, lacked an entire brigade. Furthermore, the British had reduced his cavalry division to two squadrons at Néry. His two remaining squadrons had reported increasing French activity to the west throughout the morning, including enemy columns marching on Montgé.

Gronau, an artillery officer, did not savor a fight at that moment. But German infantry doctrine holds that the best defense is an offense, and Gronau felt obliged to honor it. Holding one division in reserve, he immediately deployed his second division along a long wooded ridge that extended for five miles between Penchard on his left and St.-Soupplet on his right. Overlooking the vast plains to the west, the ridge provided an excellent vantage point from which to engage the enemy.

In late morning, Maunoury's advance guard—the Fifty-Fifth and Fifty-Sixth Reserve Divisions and the Moroccan Brigade—tramped under a blazing sun toward their line of departure for the next day's offensive, the ridge now defended by Gronau. A few kilometers short of their destination, the *poilus* fell under heavy fire from German rifles, machine guns, and artillery. The French flared out into flanking fields of beets and corn and clover. They hurried to use their 75s at once to answer the German guns. A fierce firefight followed, featuring attacks and counterattacks that lasted the rest of the day, with all forces on both sides joining the battle.

The Germans most feared the French 75-mm howitzers, which delivered a fast, accurate kind of fire called *rafale* (literally, a gust of wind)—a flurry of shrapnel shells. Their casings contained iron balls that released on impact and smothered an area with bloody agony and death. If the French 75s terrorized the Kaiser's forces, German machine guns reciprocated in kind. Most *poilus* feared nothing more than the incessant chatter of a German Maxim machine gun, as evidenced by what one French soldier wrote in 1914:

> I know nothing more depressing in the midst of battle . . . than the steady tac-tac-tac of that deadly weapon . . . There appears to be nothing material to its working. It seems to be dominated and directed by some powerful, scheming spirit of destruction.

The whiz-bangs of 75s and the tac-tac-tac of Maxims subsided at nightfall. And Gronau still controlled the ridge.

After dark, believing that he had delayed the French long enough to forestall a surprise attack on Kluck's right flank, Gronau wisely ordered a withdrawal. His corps pulled back to the heights behind the Therouanne valley, some six miles east, to a line that the French had intended to assault on September 6. Maunoury's troops gave chase under a brilliant moon, attacking enemy positions along the way, but finding most of them already abandoned by the Germans. While Galliéni in Paris was reporting "a small successful engagement near St. Soupplet," Gronau's outnumbered corps

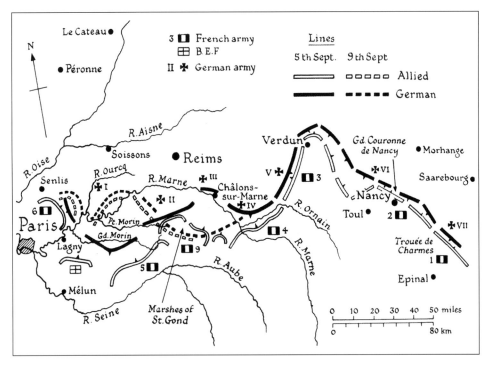

This map shows how extremely close the Germans came to taking Paris in 1914. The rivers north and east of the city helped the defense, as did heroic stands by small infantry units.

slipped away in the dark, aided by the slowing pursuit of tired *poilus*.

Kluck did not become aware of the overall strategic situation until that evening. Moltke, more alarmed than ever about the reported French buildup in Paris and equally concerned with Kluck's reluctance to abandon his southeasterly drive, sent a copy of his September 4 directive to Kluck. Lieutenant Colonel Richard Hentsch, Moltke's intelligence officer, motored to First Army H.Q. and delivered it personally to Kluck. The colonel then tried to convince the general that the German situation everywhere was more tenuous than Kluck had imagined.

So-called complete victories reported earlier by the left and center armies turned out to be only local gains. Even as they spoke, Hentsch told Kluck, Rupprecht's Sixth Army was taking heavy casualties in Lorraine, Crown Prince Wilhelm's Fifth Army and Albrecht's Fourth Army were encountering strong resistance at all points, fresh British troops had landed at Ostend with more expected, and O.H.L. now knew beyond question that the French were transferring troops to Paris. All these reasons, Hentsch concluded, made it essential for Kluck to execute Moltke's retirement order, although the movement "need not be hurried but can be carried out at complete leisure."

After hearing Hentsch's critique, Kluck agreed to swing about to face west and to withdraw as needed to realign First Army with Bülow's Second Army on his left. This movement was to be carried out over the next two days. Kluck then received Gronau's report of the day's action, in which Gronau urgently requested reinforcements. Still unconvinced of the seriousness of the French attack on his flank, Kluck sent only General Alexander von Linsingen's II Corps to aid Gronau's IV Corps, now near Monthyon.

Early on September 6, Maunoury's Sixth Army, 150,000-men strong, advanced again toward the Ourcq and by midmorning launched a vicious attack on the wooded heights now defended by Gronau's IV Corps. The *poilus* assaulted in textbook fashion, forgetting half their lessons: Sneaking forward using cover to within 800 yards of the enemy, then, line upon line, standing upright, walking at first, next trotting, and finally running full out with rifles down and bayonets fixed, they charged—into the chattering teeth of German Maxims. And line upon line, the *poilus* fell. "[T]he assault died," writes Robert B. Asprey, a principal chronicler of the battle, "and the men with it."

From the Ourcq, the battle spread all along the Western Front, tracing a great curve from due north of Paris, along the Marne and its tributaries, eastward to the heights of the fortress city of Verdun, and southeasterly almost to the Swiss border. And all along the arc, great and lesser battles raged, as astutely described by S. L. A. Marshall:

> Within this flank-to-flank collision were scores, yes, hundreds, of separate engagements, many without clear tactical purpose, most of them only indirectly bearing on actions occurring elsewhere. Men battled over worthless ground, ignoring great prizes close at hand. Artillery was fired, often wastefully, because shells were available though reliable target information was not. Generals advanced their troops who might better have spared them, fearing to miss their moment of glory. That's how war is made.

But the major battles deciding the fate of France and defining the future direction of the war were fought along the Marne and thus generally receive the lion's share of scholarly attention.

The fighting along the Ourcq had barely begun when Linsingen's II Corps joined the battle. Linsingen quickly found Gronau and relieved his junior of command. He then formed a line north of Gronau's position, west of the Ourcq. The fighting seesawed back and forth the rest of the day. Meanwhile, south of the Marne, Kluck still thought that the French assault on his right flank was no more than a spoiling action. He did not recognize it as a major counteroffensive until the next day.

On September 7, Linsingen, now heavily engaged by Maunoury's troops, called for help. Kluck sent General Sixt von Arnim's IV Corps to his relief that day—plus the III and IX Corps over the next two days. He then pulled back rapidly across the Marne and turned his entire army westward in savage counterattacks, forcing Maunoury back on the defensive, barely able to hold position.

Ferdinand Foch, in a 1916 photo. Foch later became the generalissimo in charge of all the Allied armies. In that capacity, he had heated exchanges with American General John Pershing when the United States entered the war in 1917.

Kaiser Wilhelm II elected to visit the front that day but his chauffeur soon rushed him away when the sound of French cannon and the potential nearness of French cavalry posed a threat to the German supreme commander.

In Luxembourg, as the fighting intensified far to the south, German chief of staff Helmuth von Moltke reflected

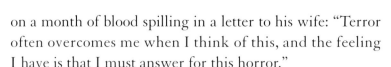

on a month of blood spilling in a letter to his wife: "Terror often overcomes me when I think of this, and the feeling I have is that I must answer for this horror."

By September 8, after three days of fighting, only the timely arrival of 6,000 French IV Corps reinforcements—rushed from Paris in 600 commandeered taxicabs by Galliéni—enabled Maunoury to check the impulsive German advance. This incident remains forever etched in the annals of French military history as "Galliéni's taxicabs."

Of Galliéni and his remarkable motorized transfer of troops, Kluck would later remark: "There was only one general who, against all the rules, would have dared to carry the fight so far from his base; unluckily for me, that man was Galliéni."

To Kluck's peril, his rapid turnabout, plus the redeployment of three corps from his left flank, opened a wide gap between himself and Bülow's Second Army. While Kluck marched northwest to the sound of the guns on his right flank, General Louis Franchet d'Esperey's Fifth Army, which had been retreating southward, also turned about and attacked the German Second Army in the widening fissure between Kluck's left flank and Bülow's right.

Field Marshal Sir John French's B.E.F., reconstituted with the addition of General Sir William Pulteney's new III Corps (Fourth Division and Nineteenth Brigade), joined with d'Esperey's army to drive a 30-mile wedge into the gap opening along the Petit Morin River. "The issue of the battle," observes Barbara Tuchman, in her classic account of August 1914, "depended on whether the Germans could succeed in crushing the wings—Maunoury and Foch—before Franchet d'Esperey and the British succeeded in exploiting the gap and pushing through the German center."

In one of the critical stages of the First Battle of the Marne, thousands of Parisian taxicabs were rounded up and used to transport Parisians to the battlefront. Here some of the taxis are shown outside the French military school at *Les Invalides* in Paris.

But both French and Franchet d'Esperey moved too slowly into the gap, lessening a great chance to break through the two armies and score a decisive victory. The French Fifth Army had begun to engage Kluck's III and IX Corps before Kluck redeployed them to the Ourcq. Franchet d'Esperey viewed their repositioning as a retreat and thus a victory, which might help to explain his sluggish advance. Militarists overwhelmingly attribute British sloth to Sir John's timidity and reluctance to cooperate with the French.

Of the B.E.F.'s cautious advance, A. J. P. Taylor writes: "The B.E.F. only covered eight miles a day, instead of the 30 miles a day which it had kept up during the retreat. Of course the men were tired; but the real failure was in leadership, which was blind and unenterprising." Taylor, one of Britain's greatest historians of the last century, was, and still is, lauded for a distinctive style and attitude in his writings. Flawed leadership in no way detracts from the solid battlefield performance of the British soldier, however, as the Tommy consistently demonstrated courage and professionalism.

Farther along the battlefront's great arc, to the southeast of Franchet d'Esperey's Fifth Army, General Ferdinand Foch's Ninth Army, while attacking north in the Marshes of St.-Gond, halted abruptly when it met strong resistance from the left flank of Bülow's Second Army. Foch's plight soon worsened dramatically. Four divisions of General Max Klemens von Hausen's German Third Army, unannounced by any preliminary artillery fire, launched a surprise bayonet attack on the Ninth Army's right flank in the early morning darkness. Terror ripped through the French ranks and the Germans shoved three of Foch's divisions back six miles onto a reserve division before he could halt their retreat and reorganize.

In his nightly report to Joffre, Foch declared: "My right is driven in, my centre is giving way, the situation is excellent, I attack." Some historians say that Foch's fabled words represent an "improved" version of his original message. But no matter what Foch wrote, he backed his words with vigorous action that morning. His *poilus* did not regain all their lost territory, but they counterattacked and plugged all the gaps in their line opened by Hausen's surprise attack. Afterward, they held fast in their positions, which amounted to a victory of sorts for Foch's exhausted troops.

In the meantime, to the east of Foch at Vitry-le-François,

General Fernand de Langle de Cary's French Fourth Army battled the Duke of Württemburg's German Fourth Army and part of Hausen's Third to a standstill. And to the right of Langle de Cary's Fourth, at Revigny in the Argonne Forest, General Maurice Sarrail's French Third Army blocked the advance of Crown Prince Wilhelm's German Fifth Army.

Southeast of Sarrail's Third, at Nancy and along the Alsace frontier, the French First and Second Armies, under Generals Auguste Dubail and Noel de Castelnau, respectively, held firm against a succession of attacks by the German Sixth and Seventh Armies led by Crown Prince Rupprecht of Bavaria and General Josias von Heeringen.

In Luxembourg, Moltke, by now in a state of near-collapse, had issued no orders for two days and remained removed, uninformed, and aloof from battlefield events. He held only a vague notion of the developing situation and apparently no intention at all of exercising any personal influence on it. Instead, he again sent Lieutenant Colonel Richard Hentsch to assess the moment.

At Châtillon-sur-Seine, as September 8 drew to a close, Joffre issued instructions for the next day. Observing that Sir John was advancing with all due caution, he ordered Maunoury's Sixth Army to keep Kluck pinned in place on the Ourcq. And he instructed Franchet d'Esperey's Fifth to close flanks with the B.E.F. and then quicken the pace. Joffre still hoped to exploit the gap between Kluck and Bülow and split their armies. But it was already too late.

Turning Point: The Battle Ends

This photograph, taken on September 9, shows French soldiers wearing captured German helmets and taking German equipment. The Marne was the first major French victory over Germans in 100 years, and France celebrated her narrow escape.

Despite Joffre's concern over the slow progress of Sir John French's B.E.F., the British had shown signs of renewed vigor on September 8. By 2:00 P.M., Haig's two divisions had opened the bridges spanning the Petit Morin to Allenby's cavalry, which quickly crossed and scattered off northward on patrol. By nightfall, after overcoming robust resistance, Sir John's right and center corps were marching toward the Marne, leaving his left corps positioned south of the Marne to lob 60-pounder high-explosive shells into German units across the river. The day's fighting cost the British 600 casualties but infused them with a new spirit and sense of purpose not felt since Le Câteau. A thunderstorm with heavy rains ended the day's action.

To the right of the B.E.F., Franchet d'Esperey's Fifth Army had advanced on the key village of Montmirail but failed to take it after two frontal assaults. The French tried another tack. General Louis Ernest de Maud'huy's XVIII Corps shifted to the left and seized a bridgehead at Marchais-en-Brie, in preparation for a strike against Bülow's right flank during the night. To the left of the B.E.F., while Kluck was planning to attack Maunoury's Sixth Army the next morning, Maunoury closed out September 8 clinging to his sector with grit and broken fingernails. That evening, he notified Joffre:

> I have all my forces engaged. . . . I am resisting on my positions. If too sharply attacked, I shall refuse my left little by little, in such a way as to march later toward the north when the pressure against me has been relieved by the offensive of the British and the Fifth Army.

Meanwhile, Hausen's Third Army continued to hammer away at Foch's battered Ninth Army to the right of Franchet d'Esperey. Such were the confrontational forces in play on Moltke's right wing when Lieutenant Colonel Richard Hentsch arrived at Bülow's Second Army Headquarters late that evening.

Hentsch, who had left O.H.L. in Luxembourg at 11:00 A.M., had first visited with the commanders of the German Fifth, Fourth, and Third Armies successively, concluding that none of the three armies needed to withdraw from its front. (The extent of Hentsch's authority is unclear since his orders from Moltke were oral and undocumented. But it is believed that Moltke spoke of "possible retirement" or "retreat" when he actually meant realignment. In any case, Hentsch felt empowered to order or approve a retreat when and if circumstances so warranted.) Despite heavy fighting on Hausen's right flank, Hentsch radioed O.H.L. that the

The solid leadership of Marshal J.C. Joffre saved France from a swift German victory.

"situation and outlook [is] entirely favorable at Third Army." He found otherwise at Second Army headquarters.

Bülow, looking tired and old beyond his 67 years, told Hentsch that "the hard combats of the last few days" had rendered his army "no longer capable of forcing a decisive victory." Moreover, he pointed out, the enemy could now readily exploit the gap between himself and Kluck, by either turning against Kluck's left wing or attacking his own right. Characterizing either eventuality as potentially catastrophic, he recommended averting "the danger by a voluntary concentric retreat of the First and Second Armies." This meant abandoning German positions that threatened Paris and retiring to the relative safety of defensive positions north of the Marne.

While Bülow and his staff weighed their options with Moltke's agent until almost midnight, Maud'huy's XVIII Corps, by then across the Petit Morin, seized control of the Courmont woods west of Marchais-en-Brie. Under cover of darkness and a rain of steel from XVIII Corps' 75s, the *poilus* launched a bayonet assault on the German outposts and trenches defending the village. Another 400 Frenchmen fell dead or wounded. But when the attackers overran the defenses, they found the trenches piled with German dead and dying and the village empty. This encroachment made Bülow's position near Montmirail untenable. "Bülow was far enough out on the limb to hear the wood cracking," comments S. L. A. Marshall. Arguably, the cracking sound heralded the turning point in the first battle of the Marne.

Early on September 9, Colonel Hentsch left Second Army headquarters to advise Kluck to retire. While Hentsch motored some 50 miles west en route to First Army H.Q., Bülow took it upon himself to act on the conclusions reached, primarily, by his staff and Hentsch. He signaled Kluck and Hausen that an aerial observer "reports long columns marching towards the Marne (the British)," and that as a consequence "Second Army is beginning retreat." He withdrew eight miles to the east and formed a line running roughly parallel to Kluck's 30-plus miles to the west. All thoughts of closing the gap disappeared into the dust stirred by thousands of German boots marching to the rear.

Moltke's right wing now stood divided effectively into three separate components, with Kluck's First Army on the right and north of the Marne, Bülow's Second Army in the center and south of the Marne but pulling back toward the Grand Morin, and Hausen's Third Army on the left standing on the Petit Morin in the Marshes of St.-Gond.

Bülow's retirement would, of course, leave Hausen's right flank vulnerable and soon force Third Army to withdraw or risk envelopment. When word of Second Army's fallback reached Hausen that morning, he began withdrawing his right wing but kept his left wing in place pending a direct order to retreat. His left wing continued battering the facing elements of Foch's Ninth Army. To inspire his troops, Foch issued a proclamation exuding pure eloquence and identifying him as a true leader:

> I ask each one of you to draw upon the last spark of energy which in its moments of supreme trial has never been denied to our race. The disorder in the enemy's ranks is the forerunner of victory. By continuing with the greatest energy the effort already begun we are certain to stop the march of the enemy and then drive him from the soil of our country. But everyone must be convinced that success belongs to him who holds out longest. The honour and safety of France are in the balance. One more effort and you are sure to win.

Shortly after Foch issued his proclamation, his commanders told him that holding position was impossible and retiring would result in complete disorder. Foch answered, "You say you cannot hold on, and that you cannot withdraw, so the only thing left is to attack." Foch ordered an attack to commence within two and a half hours. And it was to be carried out "under any and all circumstances." And the circumstances were such that Foch's ranks were continuing

Stretchers and stretcher-bearers were a common sight during and after the First Battle of the Marne. As World War I continued, the International Red Cross played a larger role in evacuating and treating the wounded. Ernest Hemingway was a Red Cross ambulance driver on the Italian front.

to yield to German thrusts at Mondement and Allemant, as well as at the critical height of Mont Août.

As the word to withdraw spread throughout the ranks of the German Second and Third Armies, Hentsch was inching his way toward First Army headquarters at Mareuil, along roads already jammed with eastward bound troops, horse-drawn artillery, ammunition and supply trains, and ambulances. Along the Ourcq, Kluck's army was now fighting as an independent entity and doing very well. With four corps in line, his First Army still outnumbered Maunoury's Sixth Army and overlapped its northern and southern flanks, keeping alive his chance of encircling the French and reversing the perilous situation that had developed on the critical German right wing.

At daybreak, General Ferdinand von Quast's IX Corps, supported by III Corps, advanced against Maunoury's Sixty-First Reserve Division in a move calculated to turn its flank and strike the defenders of Paris from the rear. When struck by Quast's forces, the French reserves took flight. By early afternoon, Kluck's two corps stood poised to sweep forward into undefended territory—and perhaps on to a decisive victory. "The balance of advantage on the Marne seemed once more to have tilted the Germans' way," wrote John Keegan. But Hentsch had arrived in Mareuil a little before noon, and the seesawing advantage was already tilting the other way again.

Kluck was off checking his troops when Hentsch reached First Army H.Q., so the young colonel reported to Kluck's chief of staff, General Hermann von Kuhl, and informed him of Bülow's predicament. While they conferred, confirmation of Hentsch's bleak assessment arrived in the form of Bülow's retirement message. Using the power allegedly vested in him by chief of the German general staff Moltke, Hentsch, a junior officer of minimal stature and questionable authority, made the most important decision of the month-old war: He ordered the retreat of the First Army. Kuhl did not dissent and Hentsch, without seeing Kluck, left to coordinate a general withdrawal. But Hentsch did not immediately notify O.H.L. of the retirements in progress.

When Kluck returned, he upheld the decision "on the grounds of the now fully changed condition of affairs, the army commander—bearing in mind the seriousness of his decision—decided on an immediate commencement of the retirement in a northern direction." One school of military thought contends that Kluck wanted to fight on but obeyed the retirement order like a good soldier. Another school insists that Kluck instead felt responsible for the German failure—because of his impulsive swing to the east of Paris and subsequent rapid advance that opened the critical gap between First and Second Armies—and that he felt more than willing to shift the blame for his own mistakes. Either way, Kluck's retreat signaled the beginning of the end of the battle.

When Moltke learned of Bülow's retirement through intercepted messages, he decided a general withdrawal was needed and presented his case to Kaiser Wilhelm II. But Wilhelm insisted on continuing the center and left offensives. Accordingly, Moltke ordered the Fourth and Fifth Armies to attack during the night of September 9th and 10th and notified Hausen's Third Army to "remain south of Châlons, ready for a new offensive."

Moltke's new order found Hausen suffering with dysentery, confused, and fearful that—with Bülow already withdrawing—his right flank might be turned if he remained in place. Hausen telephoned Hentsch, who was spending the night at Fourth Army H.Q., and explained his dilemma. Hentsch, apparently feeling more empowered than ever, assumed that Moltke, from a distance, was unaware of the true circumstances. He thus took it upon himself to authorize Hausen to withdraw at his own discretion.

Ironically, Sir John French's revitalized B.E.F., which had proved instrumental in forcing the remarkable series of German command decisions, stood halted south of the Marne, alarmed at aerial reports of a mass of German troops north of Château-Thierry. And to his right, Franchet d'Esperey's Fifth Army also made slow progress through the gap, delayed by efforts to relieve the pressure on Foch's embattled Ninth Army. The Fifth Army stopped for the night at Château-Thierry, while the Ninth Army clung precariously to its sector south of the St.-Gond marshes.

Had either the B.E.F. or the Fifth Army continued advancing through the gap that afternoon, either or both might have achieved a decisive victory over the retreating Germans and the quick end to the war that both sides had hoped for. But neither had continued, and the opportunity slipped away with the summer wind.

When night fell on September 9, neither Joffre nor his staff fully grasped the true situation, but a pleased Joffre assessed it this way: "[T]he enemy seems to have retreated, partly in the forests north of Champaubert, and on the Marne above Château-Thierry, partly on the line Etrépilly-Courchamps, where he seems to be entrenching. These forces are extended to the left by those facing the Sixth Army."

Moltke then recognized that the German offensive had failed and that a general retirement was needed along a line drawn from Noyen to Verdun. He therefore ordered his armies to withdraw and form a new front along the Aisne, the next river system above the Marne. "The lines so reached," he directed, "will be fortified and defended." These orders would be his last as chief of the German general staff.

Sporadic action occurred throughout the night along the Western Front, but when the sun's first rays gleamed over the eastern horizon on September 10, the battle ended.

After the Battle: The Might-Have-Beens of the Marne

The British steamship *Lusitania* was the pride of transatlantic passenger shipping. Germany claimed that such ships carried arms and ammunition, as well as passengers.

The Germans, with little interference from the exhausted Allied armies, completed their retirement within five days and began organizing their new positions. The legions of France, with an assist from the British, had met the Teutonic enemy at the gates of Paris and turned him away. Thus the battle—tactically indecisive—ended in a strategic victory for the Allies. It came to be known as the "Miracle on the Marne." This "miracle" cost the Allies 250,000 casualties; German losses numbered somewhat more. In about a month of war, each side had lost more than half a million men—dead, wounded, and captured.

In the battle's aftermath, Joffre, the paunchy, grandfatherly supreme commander of the Allied forces, who refused to surrender his calm in the face of uncommon chaos, emerged as the savior of France. "If we had not had him in 1914," said Ferdinand Foch, Joffre's ultimate successor, "I don't know what would have become of us."

On September 14, while Joffre was basking in the gleam of well-deserved glory, Moltke, his Prussian counterpart, descended into the darkness of a nervous collapse and was replaced by German war minister General Erich von Falkenhayn. This was also the date when the Germans reached the Aisne and began digging in.

"Trench warfare had begun," writes A. J. P. Taylor. Maneuver warfare all but ceased, except for "a last splutter of the war of movement." From September 15 through November 24 each side tried to outflank the other in what battle buffs call "the race to the sea"—a misnomer because neither side moved with great haste. Nor did either side turn a flank. The "race" ended sans winner and sans prize. "The opposing lines congealed, grew solid," continues Taylor. "The generals on both sides stared at these lines impotently and without understanding. They went on staring for nearly four years."

Although the Allies succeeded in stopping the German offensive and the drive on Paris, they stopped short of achieving a major triumph. By failing to pierce the German lines, and by not exploiting the Germans when they were in full retirement, the Allies lost the opportunity to end the war quickly. At the start of hostilities, both sides had plans in place for ending the war in only weeks—the Schlieffen Plan and Plan 17. Both failed. So, what went wrong?

As to the Schlieffen Plan, students of military strategy

generally blame Moltke and his dilution and mishandling of the German right wing for its failure. (Strategy refers to the plan, or planning, for an entire operation of a war or campaign; tactics refers to the art of positioning or maneuvering forces skillfully in battle.) For example, military historians R. Ernest Dupuy and Trevor N. Dupuy assert, "The German [Schlieffen] plan—sound and workable—failed because of the inefficiency of Moltke, who first emasculated the plan, then lost all personal touch with his army commanders and with their progress."

Other analysts submit that Schlieffen's plan was fundamentally flawed and would not have worked anyway. In pointing out the perspective of the plan's detractors, military historian and history professor Dennis E. Showalter writes:

> Well before the Marne was fought the German right wing's initial advantages in numbers and position had been steadily declining. Men and officers unaccustomed to the levels of exertion demanded by Schlieffen's grand design suffered from physical fatigue, emotional stress, and dulled wits to degrees making brilliant tactical or operational initiatives unlikely. Even had the 1st and 2nd Armies won their immediate battle, another Allied retreat would have been more likely than the dramatic destruction of the French Fifth Army and/or the B.E.F.

Still others contend that German disregard for Belgian neutrality, which brought England into the war, ranks high on the list of factors contributing to the plan's failure. And the list goes on. Armchair strategists still ponder the might-have-beens of Schlieffen's design, but only the reality of its failed execution is irrefutable.

With reference to Plan 17, the ugly stepchild of Joffre

Three months after the battle on the Marne, the war had settled into a predictable, but uncomfortable, routine of trench warfare. These are German soldiers, sleeping in wintertime.

and his staff, few would predict success for a plan that simply relied on French *élan* in the face of German Maxims. Nor would more than a few refute the appraisal of Barbara Tuchman, who attributes the plan's failure: "It had allowed the enemy to penetrate too far to be dislodged by the time the French regathered their strength at the Marne. It permitted the breakthrough that could only be stemmed, and later only contained, at a cost of the terrible drain of French manhood that was to make the war of 1914-1918 the parent of 1940." (In World War II France fell to the Germans on June 22, 1940.)

After the abysmal failure of Plan 17, only the stolid, solid leadership of Joseph J. C. Joffre and the resiliency of his armies spared France from a swift German victory— an eventuality that would have changed the face of Europe and altered the course of history. Instead, the Allies rallied at the Marne River and wrote history as it is known today. But had the first battle of the Marne—then the most decisive battle since Waterloo—ended with either side overwhelming the other, modern history books would tell a far different tale.

A quick, overpowering Allied triumph might have stayed the course of history to some degree. It still would have produced a humiliated, resentful Germany, eager to restore its ranking in the European—and ultimately the world—community, much the same as actually occurred at the end of four long, bloody years. The harsh peace terms imposed upon Germany by the Allies in the Treaty of Versailles in 1919 virtually guaranteed that Germany would march again to the sound of war drums in an effort to restore its national pride and redeem its former glory—hence an even greater global war two decades later.

Had Moltke not weakened his right wing, however, had Kluck not turned to the east, and had the Schlieffen Plan worked after all, enabling the Germans to overrun France, capture Paris, and score an overwhelming victory in six weeks, France and Britain might have sued for peace. The Germans might have then turned eastward and conquered the Russians, which might have preempted the Russian

Revolution of 1917 and even the rise of communism and the birth of the Soviet Union.

Vladimir Lenin would be remembered, if at all, as a minor political rabble-rouser. "It follows that without Lenin," comments military historian Robert Cowley, "there would have been no Stalin, no purges, no gulags, no Cold War." And without worldwide communism, there might have been no Chinese Revolution (1947-1949), no Korean War, no Cuban missile crisis or Bay of Pigs, and no Vietnam War.

On the other hand, other forms of politics, nationalism, and imperialism might have surfaced and fomented other wars. Who can predict, for example, the consequences of a victorious Germany with a world-class navy deciding to expand its imperial interests in the Pacific? It is difficult to think of an increasingly imperialistic Japan with a growing navy of its own standing idly by while Germany established an Asian sphere of influence.

A quick German victory at the Marne in 1914 and a shortened war likely would have left Germany in a position to grow and prosper. In a victorious state with a thriving economy, fewer ears might have listened to, and fewer minds might have been influenced by, the rantings of a lowly ex-corporal of the Bavarian Army. Adolf Hitler and the Nazis might never have written their sinister legacy, and 6 million Jews and others might have escaped the gas chambers of the Nazi regime. And without Hitler and his evil followers a war that claimed the lives of millions of people might have been averted.

And what of the United States? A truncated war, irrespective of the victor, would have ended long before May 7, 1915, the date when a German submarine sank the British ocean liner *Lusitania,* with 128 U.S. citizens among the 1,198 people who drowned. This act hardened

Both British and American newspapers had a field day with the sinking of the *Lusitania,* which occurred off the English coast on May 7, 1915. Nearly 1,200 people lost their lives, among them 128 Americans.

U.S. public opinion against the Germans and led to America's entry into the war when Germany renewed unrestricted submarine warfare in 1917.

"If an armistice had come at the end of 1914," notes Robert Cowley, "our country would have remained for years what it was then: a crude, boisterous, and not always charming provincial cousin. No American boys would have crossed our Rubicon, the Atlantic." Had America and American soldiers not become bloodied in the first global war it might also have remained aloof from the second. The obvious question then becomes: could, or would, America have become the superpower that it is today? And if not, what would life be like for

When the war ended, the Allied peacemakers were adamant that Germany not be allowed to rearm. German aircraft were dismantled and scrapped, as was the German fleet, built at such expense prior to the war.

Americans today? Better? Worse? Who can say?

The might-have-beens of the Marne feed upon themselves. Each speculation gives rise to another, with the scope of each supposition limited only by the imagination of the speculator. Therein dwells the stuff of military fantasy. The reality of the Marne is that the failure of either side to score a quick victory condemned the combatants to four more years of horror and mass killing in the trenches of the Western Front; four years that decimated a generation of young men and inflicted scars on the human psyche that still endure today.

Within this frame of reference, the first battle of the Marne—the first great battle of modern warfare—changed the world forever.

After the war, former B.E.F. liaison officer Edward Spears wrote of his experiences. Remembering how he felt four days after the First Marne ended, he scribed: "I am deeply thankful that none of those who gazed across the Aisne on September 14 had the faintest glimmer of what was awaiting them."

1871

May 10   Treaty of Frankfort: Franco-Prussian War ended; France paid reparations and ceded northeast provinces of Alsace and Lorraine to Germany.

1914

June 28   Serbian activist Gavrilo Princip assassinated Austro-Hungarian Archduke Franz Ferdinand and his spouse in the Bosnian capital of Sarajevo.

July 5   Kaiser Wilhelm II pledged to support a hostile Austrian action against Serbia.

July 23   Austria presented a 10-point ultimatum to Serbia and demanded a reply within 48 hours.

July 28   Austria-Hungary declared war on Serbia.

July 31   Russia and Austria-Hungary mobilized; Italy declared its neutrality; Germany demanded the cessation of Russian mobilization; Russia refused.

1914

JUNE   JULY

July 28
Austria-Hungary
declares war
on Serbia

June 28
Serbian activist Gavrilo Princip assassinates
Austro-Hungarian Archduke Franz Ferdinand and
his spouse in the Bosnian capital of Sarajevo

Timeline

August 1   Germany declared war on Russia and began to mobilize; French mobilization commenced that same day.

August 2   Germany demanded right of passage across Belgian territory.

August 3   Germany declared war on France and German troops entered Belgium.

August 4   Great Britain declared war on Germany.

August 5   German forces reached the Belgian fortress-city of Liège.

August 12   British Expeditionary Force (B.E.F.) began landing at Le Havre, Boulogne, and Rouen, France.

August 14-22   Battle of Lorraine.

August 16   Liège fell to Germans.

August 20-25   Battle of the Ardennes.

August 22   B.E.F. arrived at Mons-Condé Canal, Belgium.

August 22-23   Battle of the Sambre (or Charleroi).

August 1
Germany declares war on Russia and begins to mobilize; French mobilization commences that same day

August 3
Germany declares war on France and German troops enter Belgium

August 22-23
Battle of the Sambre (or Charleroi)

August 23
Battle of Mons

August 25-27
Battle of Le Câteau

August 31
General Alexander von Kluck shifts his First Army eastward and thereby scraps the last vestiges of the Schlieffen Plan.

AUGUST   **SEPTEMBER**

August 4
Britain declares war on Germany

August 14-22
Battle of Lorraine

August 20-25
Battle of the Ardennes

August 29
Battle of Guise (or St.-Quentin)

August 24
Plan 17 (French battle plan) fails; Allied supreme commander General Joseph Joffre begins to plan new strategy

September 5-10
The First Battle of the Marne

September 2
French government moves from Paris to Bordeaux, leaving the defense of Paris to General Joseph-Simon Galliéni, while French troops pour into the capital city

August 23	Battle of Mons.
August 24	Belgian fortress-city of Namur fell to Germans; B.E.F. retreated from Mons; Plan 17 (French battle plan) failed; Allied supreme commander General Joseph Joffre began to plan new strategy.
August 25-27	Battle of Le Câteau.
August 27	General Hellmuth von Moltke, chief of the German general staff, updated German orders and began to erode the original German strategy of the Schlieffen Plan.
August 29	Battle of Guise (or St.-Quentin).
August 30	German monoplane dropped leaflets over Paris demanding Allied surrender; a gap began to open between the German First and Second Armies.
August 31	General Alexander von Kluck shifted his First Army eastward and thereby scrapped the last vestiges of the Schlieffen Plan.
September 2	French government moved from Paris to Bordeaux, left the defense of Paris to General Joseph-Simon Galliéni, while French troops poured into the capital city.
September 5-10	The First Battle of the Marne.
September 14	General Moltke replaced by General Erich von Falkenhayn; German troops began digging in along the Aisne, a precursor to four years of trench warfare.

Chapman, Guy, *A Passionate Prodigality: Fragments of an Autobiography.* New York: Holt, Rinehart and Winston, 1966.

Clausewitz, Carl von, *On War.* Baltimore, MD: Penguin Books, 1968.

Corvisier, André, and John Childs, eds., and Chris Turner, trans., *A Dictionary of Military History and the Art of War.* Cambridge, MA: Blackwell Publishers, 1993.

Cowley, Robert, and Geoffrey Parker, eds., *The Reader's Companion to Military History.* Boston: Houghton Mifflin, 1996.

Davis, Paul K., *100 Decisive Battles: From Ancient Times to the Present.* New York: Oxford University Press, 1999.

Eggenberger, David, *An Encyclopedia of Battles: Accounts of Over 1,560 Battles from 1479 B.C. to the Present.* Mineola, NY: Dover Publications, 1985.

Hansen, Arlen J., *Gentlemen Volunteers: The Story of American Ambulance Drivers in the Great War, 1914-1918.* New York: Arcade Publishing, 1996.

Haythornthwaite, Philip J., *The World War I Source Book.* London: Arms and Armour, 1994.

Keegan, John, *The Face of Battle.* New York: Penguin Books, 1985.

Kennett, Lee, *The First Air War 1914-1918.* New York: The Free Press, 1991.

Messenger, Charles, *The Century of Warfare: Worldwide Conflict from 1900 to the Present Day.* New York: HarperCollins, 1995.

Parker, Geoffrey, ed., *The Cambridge Illustrated History of Warfare.* New York: Cambridge University Press, 1995.

Perrett, Bryan, *Crucial Conflicts in History from 1469 BC to the Present.* London: Arms and Armour Press, 1992.

Saunders, Anthony, *Weapons of the Trench War 1914-1918.* Phoenix Mill, UK: Sutton Publishing, 1999.

Taylor, A. J. P., *The Struggle for Mastery in Europe.* London: The Folio Society, 1998.

Young, Peter, *A Dictionary of Battles 1816-1976.* New York: Mayflower Books, 1977.

PICTURE CREDITS

EARLE RICE JR. is a former senior design engineer and technical writer in the aerospace industry. After serving nine years with the U.S. Marine Corps, he attended San Jose City College and Foothill College on the San Francisco Peninsula. He has been writing fulltime since 1993 and had written more than 30 books for young adults. Earle is a member of the Society of Children's Book Writers and Illustrators (SCBWI); the League of World War I Aviation Historians and its U.K.-based sister organization, Cross & Cockade International, the United States Naval Institute, and the Air Force Association.